Making Work Systems Better

Making Work Systems Better

A Practitioner's Reflections

Luc Hoebeke
International Institute for Organisational
and Social Development, Leuven, Belgium

JOHN WILEY & SONS
Chichester • New York • Brisbane • Toronto • Singapore

Other Wiley Editorial Offices

John Wiley & Sons, Inc., 605 Third Avenue,
New York, NY 10158-0012, USA

Jacaranda Wiley Ltd, 33 Park Road, Milton
Queensland 4064, Australia

John Wiley & Sons (Canada) Ltd, 22 Worcester Road,
Rexdale, Ontario M9W 1L1, Canada

John Wiley & Sons (SEA) Pte Ltd, 37 Jalan Pemimpin #05-04,
Block B, Union Industrial Building, Singapore 2057

Library of Congress Cataloging-in-Publication Data

Hoebeke, Luc.
    Making work systems better : a practitioner's reflections
/ Luc Hoebeke.
        p.   cm.
    Includes bibliographical references and index.
    ISBN 0-471-94248-0
    1. Organizational behavior.   2. Organizational effectiveness.
I. Title.
HD58.7.H627   1994
    658.4—dc20   93–30452
                                                                CIP
British Library Cataloguing in Publication Data

A catalogue record for this book is available from the British Library

ISBN 0-471-94248-0

Typeset in 10/12pt Palatino from author's disks by Text Processing Department,
John Wiley & Sons Ltd, Chichester
Printed and bound in Great Britain by Biddles Ltd, Guildford, Surrey

To both my parents,
who died while this book was born

Contents

Contents _____ ix

CHAPTER 9
Annotated Bibliography and Conclusions

CHAPTER 10
Synopsis and Glossary

Index

Foreword

Sir Geoffrey Vickers once said to me, and he was in his mid-eighties at the time, that he no longer had time to carry on reading any book with which he found himself in agreement! Only if the book did some rearranging of his mental furniture did he continue to read it. I think that Sir Geoffrey would have stayed with Luc Hoebeke's book through to the end, because though it is informed by Vickers' notion of 'appreciative systems' (as well as by the work of Beer, Checkland and Jaques) it offers a unique view of the process of management which will help to rearrange some mental furniture for most of its readers. When I read the early manuscript it was like coming across a copse of green trees in the otherwise rather arid landscape of organisation and management theory, not least because it was not simply a theoretical work; it was the result of deep reflection on the relation between our experience of managing and the mental constructions we develop to make sense of that experience. Luc Hoebeke is the epitome of Donald Schon's 'reflective practitioner'.

That I am personally sympathetic to the process view of management expressed here is no doubt due to my own experience in the field. I was at first a physical chemist, taking part in the game to define Nature's regularities which natural scientists play. Then I became a technologist in science-based industry and quickly learnt that although the science remains unaltered, the value system which lies behind the activity of an industrial scientist is very different. What I had been doing previously in the Physical Chemistry Laboratory at Oxford made sense only in terms of a value system which assumed that new knowledge is an ultimate good, taken as given, valued for its own sake. What I was doing in industry made sense only in terms of a different assumption, namely that the generation of wealth is an ultimate good, the value of which is taken as given. This I could understand. But when I became a manager I found my situation much more problematical. What was the nature of this strange and difficult activity of 'managing'? What were its values?

At that point I discovered the existence of a literature calling itself 'Management Science', and imagined that it would tell me, an ex-scientist, now a manager, just what I needed to know. Imagine my surprise when I found that the textbooks (and I now know that the student texts, in particular, reflect only dimly what the best practitioners do) were simply irrelevant to everything I was doing, day by day, as a manager.

Later on, as I began to read the organisational management literature, I found that it too failed to reflect much of the lived texture of organisational life as members of organisations experience it. The lists of academic publishers were heavy with 700-page tomes on management which simply took as given the conventional wisdom that organisations were goal-seeking entities functionally structured to achieve their succession of goals.

By then my colleagues and I were deep into a programme of action research in organisations in which we tried to use systems thinking to help tackle the kind of ill-structured problematical situations with which managers have somehow to cope. From these experiences we were led to a process view of management, to the view that the answer to the old question: does form follow function or function follow form? was, at least for managers, that structure *ought* not to be prime, but *ought* to follow from decisions on what processes were crucial and how they should be organised.

When I began to work with Luc Hoebeke, on an education programme for executives which he had helped to create, I discovered that he and I were labouring in the same vineyard, and it is a pleasure to welcome a vintage product from his work.

Wisely he does not talk of organisations but of 'work systems' and the way in which the processes they enact are shaped into coherent patterns by the act of managing: managing is, above all, concerned with attributing meaning to process patterns. This is a long way from the conventional wisdom, and, by establishing a basic way of conceptualising process which can be applied recursively, Luc takes us successively from the process level concerned with a time span of a day or two through to the cultural, even spiritual, levels at which the relevant time span is 50 years and beyond.

This is a book worth reading and re-reading, a book that will cause you to think about the frameworks by which you personally create meaning for yourself. You cannot ask more of a book than that.

Peter Checkland
November 1993

Preface

The plan to write this book arose after I had written my first during a sabbatical leave in the second half of 1991. Its structure and basic elements were completed in three weeks during the spring of 1992. As it was then, it was unreadable: it was merely a sequence of definitions, with a minimum of comments and examples. Nevertheless, I showed it to several friends and explained the framework to my colleagues in IOD (The International Institute for Organizational and Social Development). They received it with interest and curiosity and stimulated me to develop the basic ideas further.

Therefore I wrote a second draft and sent it to Diane Taylor of John Wiley & Sons, who had shown interest in the manuscript of my first book but correctly declared it to be unpublishable by Wiley. Ultimately it will be issued by an artbook publisher. The second draft appeared to Diane Taylor rather more palatable than the first, in that four reviewers made the effort to read it and sent me very valuable comments. To one of them, I am indebted for the clarification between the concepts of process level and recursion level. Another forced me to develop more clearly the concept of the span of relations. What had formerly appeared to be only a digression from the general discourse now became a central concept of the whole argument. A third reviewer correctly advised me to add the application sections to their corresponding chapters instead of having a separate chapter of their own.

However, I am mostly indebted to the perseverance of Diane Taylor at Wiley and to Peter Checkland of Lancaster University, and to their patience with me for making the book much more readable and thus publishable. Diane helped me even through the very difficult marketing hurdle, which every author has to pass when publishing for the first time.

Last, but not least, I am indebted to Ron Markillie for reviewing the whole text and for making it much more acceptable to English-speaking readers.

I cannot omit those people who have had to bear my fluctuating moods while I was writing, sometimes full of energy, sometimes despairingly. My wife and children know all about the book without ever having read it.

Here should follow a very long list of people who, consciously or unconsciously, have contributed in one way or another to the development of the framework of the book. But I am most grateful to my colleagues at IOD, to my students and to my clients, who have permitted me to try the framework in practice. Sometimes they have been as much surprised as I at the discoveries, agreeable and disagreeable, we made together. They are the first witnesses of the generative character of the framework. For them and for me the world of work has become much more transparent and simple. This makes working life not necessarily more simplistic but at least more worth living.

L.H.
1993

Chapter 1

Background and Purpose

Organizational problems are too simple to deserve much effort. Problems of centralization and decentralization, responsibility and delegation, and management information and control conceal many more interesting issues. As an organization and management consultant I prefer to work on issues worth exploration and intervention in a creative and thus profoundly human way. Why people work, how they deal with the tension of belonging to and working in different work systems, how they cope with the dilemmas of destruction and creation, life and death at work, how they express their sexuality in work, these have much more impact on their life, on the tools they design and use and on the fruits of their endeavours than management and organizational aspects. Somewhere organization scholars got their priorities wrong when they started to focus primarily upon organizations, their structure and their management instead of upon meaningful work.

Out of 100 of my students who already had work experience and whom I asked to draw a model of their organization, 90 had only the hierarchical organization chart, the pyramid, in their repertoire. When I ask them to name the clients for whom they were working, 80 referred to higher management levels, and when I asked them to define the results of their contributions, the products and services they were delivering, 50 mentioned activities and not outputs. The implicit world view that they seemed to have about their work was that only the continuity of the organization, its hierarchical relations and structure were important. The most common reference to the organizational environment (80%) was about the competition. Although there is much lip-service paid in the business literature to customers and clients, in practice, organizational language is used to exclude them. Most of these students were nevertheless aware of the discrepancy between their real working experience and the organizational language they used.

The need for a language which refers mainly to the work and its meaning in the world we are creating and destroying was the main reason for writing this book. Using this language helps me and my clients to focus more quickly on relevant organizational issues which the current language permits us to evade too easily.

The practical reasons which caused me to write are threefold:

(1) I am meeting an increasing number of organizational practitioners who are aware that the current organizational models are irrelevant for explaining the performance of the organizations with whom they are working. They see clearly that this performance is better understood when they consider work systems as systems of more or less loosely coupled self-regulated semi-autonomous networks rather than static hierarchical pyramids. However, they lack a framework for consciously stimulating this attitude towards networks.

(2) I am urged by younger colleagues, students and clients alike, to transfer the framework which I use to diagnose organizations. Apparently I seem to be able to discern patterns which for me have become self-evident but are revelations for them and permit them to intervene in organizational issues that were previously either undecidable or even beyond explanation.

(3) Until now, I could refer those who asked for elements of the framework I am developing to the works of Peter Checkland, Stafford Beer and Elliott Jaques. But apparently I started to internalize their concepts so strongly that a book of my own has developed. I do not think that there is a worthwhile cost-benefit ratio in forcing my students and colleagues through the same process. Nevertheless, I suggest strongly, once they have started to use the following framework, that they go back to these authors who were the origins of my own thinking about organizations.

I am indebted to Peter Checkland for two major elements of this book:

- I started to work much more consciously with the fact that a framework and the reality to which it is applied should never be identified, that a map is never the territory. The framework is a language for debate and interpretation, not for dogma. Peter labels this the epistemological stance.
- His definition of a human activity system (HAS) covers completely my definition of a work system. This concept helped me to define relevant boundaries around human activities, instead of the formal organizational boundaries, which are mostly taken for granted.

I am also indebted to Stafford Beer for the two major foundations of this book:

- He helped me to overcome my disillusion with (positivistic) science, when as an engineer I was confronted with its irrelevance in Latin America in the late 1960s. His *Decision and Control* and *Brain of the Firm* convinced me that logical rigour could still be valuable in human problems as long as it is related to one's own sense of elegance or beauty. It helps to keep Occam's razor in mind when confronted with the pseudo-complexity of most of what is now called management science. Reductionism has stopped being a 'dirty' word, and its necessity and limitations became operational for me through my work with the Viable Systems Model (VSM).

- I was fortunate to have struggled with Beer's VSM before I started to read organizational and management theory, which comes from the social sciences. When relevant, this school of thought gives insight mainly into the relational aspects of human work, while the VSM helped me to understand the activities performed in and by organizations. When I read the socio-technical literature I was able to connect immediately the empirical understanding of this school to the theoretical elegance and insights of the VSM. They are still guiding me in my endeavours.

Elliott Jaques is the latest of the influential authors with whom I became acquainted. Although I am very critical of the way he takes existing organizational structures for granted, his discovery of the 'Forms of Time' enabled me to discover a final link in the framework I develop further:

- Hierarchies are in the minds of people and are related to their intentional time perspective. From my control engineering background I was aware that time is an essential operator in all kinds of self-regulated systems. How this operator is directly linked with one's own personality, or how each individual has his or her own time horizon and applies it to human activities was a major discovery. As a practitioner I discovered my tendency to structure my interventions in organizations as a function of my own time perspective, and in this way I was able to understand my shortcomings and my successes. This also allowed me to seek colleagues who were able to broaden the range of time perspectives relevant for whole-system interventions.

After this tribute, it is also worth examining what my working through of these authors has added to the seminal work they did:

- By using the concepts of Peter Checkland I discovered certain generic patterns of Human Activity Systems. These patterns seem to help my clients and students to define more easily the systems with which they are working and their output characteristics. It helps them also to define their work systems despite the formal organizational boundaries, which in many cases are also mental blocks. I transformed these patterns into

a typology of HAS in order to facilitate the use of Soft Systems Methodology.
- The elegance and the rigour of Beer's VSM also seems to be the major
  obstacle to its use. I think that there are two reasons why the use of the VSM
  generates so much resistance in people confronted with this way of
  understanding their organizations. The fact that more attention is paid to
  what Beer calls organizational pathologies and their diagnosis is not
  very helpful for putting effort into improvements. Asking someone to
  stop smoking because of his or her health while he or she is not feeling
  ill does not often lead to the requisite action, in spite of being a relevant
  diagnosis. I experienced much more success with the model when I was
  able to point out why a work system was still viable in spite of apparently
  major variety imbalances revealed by the VSM. Improving the variety
  amplifiers and filters already in place in the system is an easier task than
  designing completely new ones. Moreover, Beer and some of his followers
  are still too easily seduced to apply the VSM to 'big' systems. Later I will
  develop the hypothesis that, due to the constraints of the 'span of
  relations', big systems are intrinsically not viable except as ideological
  social constructs borne by a limited number of people. The Viable
  Systems Model becomes a Virtual Systems Model, useful for debates but
  not, as such, able to be operationalized by the same people. Beer refers
  to a power caucus many times. My experience of a power caucus is its
  powerlessness once it aims to transform its virtual world into a real one
  and the VSM may seduce its members along that path.
- It may seem paradoxical that Elliott Jaques, who has provided me with
  the keystone of the framework which I will develop, is also an author
  who has, in my opinion, a poor understanding of work systems. His
  background as a psychiatrist may have misguided him. While his
  understanding of the individual cognitive capabilities, measured by
  one's work capacity, is extremely relevant and valuable, the same
  understanding limits his view on organizations to relations between
  managers and subordinates. In people's minds the hierarchies become
  embodied in real people and the way they relate. The reason for their
  relation is not dealt with. I hope that using his concepts to make a
  typology of activities, instead of a typology of relations, may clarify
  some of the misunderstanding and the resistance he has caused and is
  still causing. I also hope that my story of the four stonemasons (see
  Section 3.2) gives an alternative to his pyramidal meritocratic world
  view, perpetuating the division between doers and thinkers, and placing
  the latter on top of the pyramid.

Now I can state the aims of the conceptual framework, which I developed based on the works of these authors.

This book aims to describe a conceptual framework that is relevant for understanding and intervening in the task-related issues of work systems.

Let us look first at the various elements of this sentence. A conceptual framework is a coherent system of concepts which permit its users to communicate creatively about a given domain of experience, in this case the domain of work systems. People who are sharing a common task can use the conceptual framework to debate it between themselves before combining in a joint effort to influence it. The framework permits description and prescription alike.

One of the words I use frequently is 'relevance'. A conceptual framework is neither true nor false: it is a means of conveying truths or falsehoods and the fuzzy area between both. It can be used and abused; both are aspects of human creativity. The relevance of the framework will be assessed when its descriptive and prescriptive power is put to work for good or bad.

But the discovery of what is true and false, of what is good and bad does not belong to the domain of the framework itself. At its extreme, it can be used descriptively and prescriptively for the production and distribution of addictive drugs and for the organization of an aid campaign for the victims of an earthquake. The framework is relevant for all kinds of human activity. But it is essentially anti-bureaucratic: i.e. human activities are referred to real people and not to anonymous superordinate entities such as gods, institutions, economy, goals, the Organization or Collective Man in whatever form. *The value behind the framework and part of its aims is to relate human activities again with identifiable human beings.*

Now it is important to touch upon the limitations of the framework. As Peter Checkland has pointed out, human activity systems or work systems can be regarded as a set of activities and a set of relations between the people doing them (Figure 1.1). The framework I propose deals *mainly* with *the set of activities.* I mentioned earlier that for me the most fascinating part of my work is the relations between the people involved in activities and their interactions. That is the part where intuition and art play an important role: trying to conceptualize this aspect too much easily leads to 'social engineering' and inadvertently limits the freedom of creating new behavioural repertoires. The set of activities is easier to 'objectify', i.e. it lends itself more easily to a coherent system of concepts. For me, it is that part of my experience which can be conceptualized with more rigour and which can help people to understand why they are collaborating and competing at the same time to create meaning together.

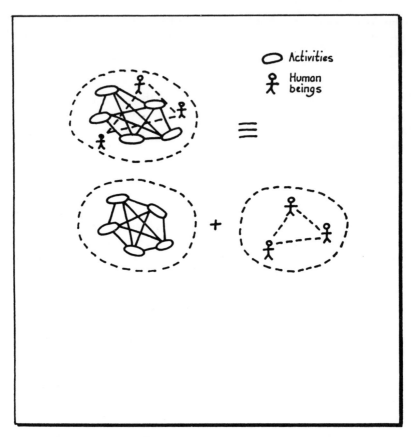

Figure 1.1 A work system or a Human Activity System (HAS)

I want to make a final preliminary comment on the use of the term 'work system', instead of 'organization'. Too often I have seen how the word 'organization' is loaded with formal connotations of status, prerogatives, ownership and power, and omits the activity aspect. Even legally, organizational and institutional boundaries are defined around people, not activities.

As a patient in a hospital I do not belong formally to the hospital payroll, while my contribution is essential to fulfil the basic purpose of that hospital: to keep me alive, until I am able to live outside it. From the viewpoint of work I belong to the hospital work system. Formally, I am a patient and someone pays for the services I receive.

During a workshop session in a management programme, the hotel bellboy came in to deliver a fax to one of the participants. I could make my point clear by mentioning that the bellboy made a contribution to a work system of the company of the manager without being on its payroll.

Regarding the set of activities, legal and formal boundaries are mostly irrelevant. As novelists say, all resemblance between organizational boundaries and work system boundaries is purely coincidental. This will be your major discovery when you use the framework I will present. To help you to make that shift in perception, I use the term 'work system' instead of 'organization'. Work system refers to work, to a system of meaningful activities.

One last reading hint: the definitions of the concepts are displayed in italic type, while illustrative examples are sans serif type. The examples I use come from my own experience and from my reading of the literature. I interpret both sources by means of the framework which I develop. In no way can the examples from my reading be thought of as arguments *ex autoritate* for the framework. The examples are no more than illustrations of how I look at what I experience and what I read. I leave it to the reader to sort out their relevance.

Chapter 2 defines the basic concepts of the framework. Chapter 3 uses these concepts to introduce the four domains of activities. Chapters 4 to 7 develop then further the conceptual framework for the four activity domains. Chapter 8 tries to help the reader to start to use the framework. It does so in two ways: by giving some practical hints and by raising a series of controversial issues, which can be derived directly from the framework. Chapter 9 gives a final comment and a brief annotated bibliography. Chapter 10 is a synopsis of the whole book and places the most important definitions in their context. It replaces an alphabetical glossary.

Chapter 2

Basic Concepts of the Framework

2.1 CONCEPTS REFERRING TO THE WORK SYSTEM ITSELF

2.1.1 The Work System

A work system is a purposeful definition of the real world in which people spend effort in more or less coherent activities for mutually influencing each other and their environment.

This sentence requires some explanation. Defining a work system means making a decision about which unit it is relevant to discuss, and which unit the framework, which will be further developed, should be used for. Never confuse a definition with the mysterious reality beneath it. As with all choices, defining a work system requires a decision and as with all decisions, it requires a purpose, an intention. I do not wish to elaborate on whom is deciding or for what purpose. I only want to point out that the debate about this question can never be avoided if the definition has to lead to joint action. All parties involved in a joint action must at least agree with the definition of a work system .

The actions taken for improving the operations of a public library will be quite different if it is defined as a work system for keeping books in an orderly manner or as one that lends books to readers.

A work system is the basic unit of our framework. Most other concepts will be attributes of work systems. It is essential that you name the work system that you define.

In the previous example it is practical in both cases to call the work system a public library.

But evidently a name is not sufficient. Peter Checkland deserves credit for having systematically studied the elements of the definition of a work system, so that the selection and its purpose become more transparent for the parties interested in using the definition. Peter Checkland calls the central part of a definition a transformation process.

2.1.2 Transformation Process

A transformation process expresses a basic purpose behind the work system and transforms a specified input into a specified output. The output must contain the input which has been transformed during the process.

We can see in the purchasing work system of a production plant three transformation processes which may not immediately be recognized as such. Material transformation processes are obvious enough. Organizational ones highlight more the need to select them carefully:

- A purchasing work system transforms the need for materials in production into a fulfilment of these needs.
- A purchasing work system transforms the needs of the plant for working relations with material suppliers into a fulfilment of these needs by supplier–purchaser contracts.
- A purchasing work system transforms the need for the long-term availability of strategic materials into a virtual fulfilment of these needs by potential suppliers and/ or potential substitute materials.

Let me first stress again the difference between a work system and an organizational unit. The first definition implies contributions from those people who generate the need for materials, from those who produce, store, handle and transport them. The second implies contributions from the legal and financial competences on both sides, the customer company and the supplier company, and most probably from the designers and users of the materials to reach an agreement on material specifications. The third implies a complete intelligence network to track the evolution and trends in the materials market.

In no case are the organizational boundaries of the purchasing work system the same as those of a common purchasing department. But in any purchasing department one will find people who contribute to at least one of the three transformation processes.

All three processes are adequate expressions of the purpose of the work system, which we call the purchasing work system. Nevertheless, the nature of the required activities for making each process happen is quite different. These differences appear in the explicit mentioning of the inputs and the outputs of the processes.

In the first definition we can visualize all those activities that are needed to generate a material flow and the necessary information flow to make it happen. In contrast, the second definition refers to contracts, the legal, engineering and financial conditions which have to be fulfilled to make the first process feasible. These activities belong to the domain of procurement, as Michael Porter[1] calls it in his book on strategic competitiveness. The third definition refers to the development of the conditions in which suppliers with whom contracts are feasible can be discovered.

Through the example we can add a new concept .

2.1.3 Process Level

A process of a higher order is one whose output creates conditions for one of a lower order. Processes can be differentiated in a hierarchy. To avoid confusion with what is seen in organizational terms as hierarchical levels we call this the process level (Figure 2.1).

A plant manager has a well-defined hierarchical position in his organization: his status and pay depend on it. Now suppose that the same plant manager is telephoning a supplier to send a certain material urgently. In this activity he is contributing to the process of the lowest process level by which we previously defined the purchasing work system . When he is dining with a colleague from the supplier organization, both are contributing to the next higher process level of the same purchasing work system. They are creating goodwill to come to an agreement, which leads to a contract. When the plant manager visits an industrial fair and inquires about the characteristics of a material, which may eventually replace one of the base materials of the products made in his plant, he is contributing to the third process, one level higher than the second one.

Hierarchical position and authority are linked to the relations between people in organizations, to their prerogatives and their benefits, and not to the contributions they make. I invite the reader to apply the concepts developed so far to describe problems of delegation of responsibility, of centralization versus decentralization and other structural problems.

Although the action taken by our plant manager in the first case will not be found in his job description it can be very relevant: in some way he is functionally redundant to the person(s) who has the job description of chasing materials. For one reason or another he is replacing this person.
Very often, 'higher' managers feel obliged to take on the tasks of salespeople or purchasers because of an unwritten law which requires that people of equal status should negotiate contracts. Relational aspects and work aspects are confused. Blaming the manager for not doing his or her job and not being able to delegate is as irrelevant here as sending a subordinate because of the tenets of delegation, and thus running the risk of jeopardizing the negotiation.

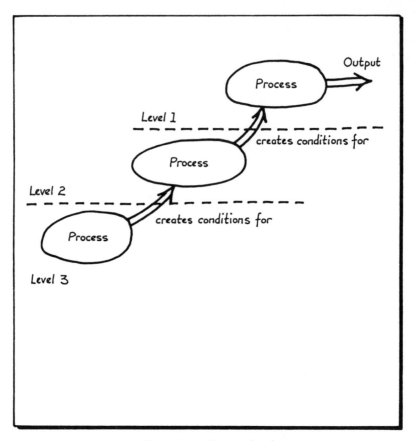

Figure 2.1 Process levels

I hope that this illustration helps the reader, like all colleagues who start to use this framework, to discover that, conceptually, organizational life becomes much simpler once you identify a person with a function. Nevertheless, this does not mean that the issues of prerogatives and power, authority and delegation become more tractable. They can be distinguished from the domain of job and function descriptions.

Most people contribute normally to processes on three different successive process levels. They are bound to lose relevance when they deploy activities which go beyond three levels. This is due to the limited information-processing capabilities of a human being. As Beer[2] wrote ironically: for someone to be able to grasp the complexity of the sum of all the levels of an organization, the volume of his or her head should grow exponentially with the number of levels he or she encompasses. As I mentioned earlier, it is impossible to infer to which processes people contribute on the basis of their organizational position. It is only by defining the processes and their outputs that their activities can be discussed.

2.1.4 Contributions of People

We call contributions those activities of people belonging to a work system which can be seen as helping to realize the defined output of a process. The process level defines the level of the contribution at the same time.

People can be held responsible only for their own individual contributions, not for the contribution of someone else. Responsibility can never be delegated. Conversely, only if one person makes all the contributions necessary to generate the output of a process, is it meaningful to assign the responsibility for the output to that person. For all other processes, the responsibility is shared by all those making contributions. For formal reasons it may be useful to hold someone who is contributing to the process accountable for the output of that process. He or she is the person to be contacted by the external parties influenced by the results of the process.

2.1.5 Responsibility and Accountability

One can be held responsible only for one's own contributions to a process. As a formal simplifying mechanism it may be useful to have someone accountable for the process and its output. In this way, responsibilities and accountabilities become nominally known. Anonymous entities such as organizations, departments, institutions, groups, governments, etc. can be held neither responsible or accountable.

Empirically, one person can be held accountable for three different processes on one process level. Thus the maximum number of accountabilities is limited to nine: three processes times three levels.

This may seem a rather serious limitation. But first it should be understood that a contribution is defined by a result, an output, and not by all the activities which lead to that output. Second, and more importantly, the framework I am developing uses definitions as choices, as purposeful selections, not as an exhaustive inventory of all that people do in 'real life'.

A group of six project managers suffered from work overload or, in their terms, from a lack of time. Because they were reflective practitioners and wanted to do something about their problem, they started to make an inventory of all their activities and the percentage of time they devoted to each. The inventory required about twenty pages and was not helping them to improve their situation: the inventory was a material expression of their overload problem. But I urged them to compare their respective lists and to discuss their reduction into three major dimensions, which generated an output *sui generis*. In this way they were helped to transform a problem of a lack of time into one of setting priorities.

The three times three accountability list is the minimal critical specification of whatever job description, work contract, responsibility and accountability description, when there is a need to formalize it and to make it public and transparent. The person accountable for the process and its results is the one who assesses the various contributions needed from the people involved in the process. He or she should know these persons individually. There is no need to formalize all the contributions of one person to all the processes in which he or she is involved. The formalization is only useful for those processes whose output cannot be created through a face-to-face group, i.e. where the interpersonal relations also have to be contractually defined. This principle has the same validity for the President of the United States as for a gardener in the White House. The only difference lies in the nature of the processes to which they are contributing.

It has become a routine for me to start my contracts with clients with my perception of their desired results, and further to specify my contributions towards these results. In fact, when I convey in this way why I should collaborate with them my degree of freedom in what and how I do things becomes greater. Hence, this enables me to focus upon the relevance of my interventions instead of upon their nature.

It is clear that such a reduction into nine small sentences which, at most, take only one A4 sheet (see Table 2.1) for any job description is very different from the normal way, in which specialist job analysts and salary system consultants can spend an enormous amount of time and money to arrive at an unclear so-called 'objective' set of job descriptions. The reasons why it is necessary to go into these rituals are :

- Job and function descriptions are more concerned with the relations, especially those of power and status, between people than with the activities to be fulfilled. The language of tasks is used in an improper way when speaking of human relations.
- As power and status relations are generating social comparison and, as such, have a political character, i.e. are related to value judgements stemming from different value systems, job and function descriptions are intrinsically conflict-ridden. In our organizational bureaucratic organizations, one of the ways in which we deal with healthy conflicts is by resolving them by means of a 'scientific methodology'.

Table 2.1 Contribution form

Process level 1: Desired output
Contribution 1:
Transforming A into B for C (customer)
Transforming D into E for F
Transforming G into H for I
Contribution 2:
Transforming ...
Process level 2: Desired condition for process level 1
Contribution 4: ...
Process level 3: Desired condition for process level 2
Contribution 7: ...

- This methodology (if workable) cannot resolve the conflict. For this reason, it leads to ambiguity and lack of clarity so that, unseen, the conflict can continue. The rituals of annual performance appraisals and the subsequent decisions on salary are self-regulating but inefficient mechanisms for dealing with the intrinsic conflict.

All this may seem common sense. Nevertheless, the identification of persons with functions is the most common source of misunderstanding in organizations. Function is a static positioning concept, while contributions are dynamic. Once the language of contributions is used many ambiguities disappear: prerogatives and status become part of the relational dimension of organizations and no longer interfere with the activities to be performed. This is stated very simply here. In practice, it is more difficult to deal with the transparency created by this approach. Sometimes this transparency reveals that the Emperor is wearing no clothes.

2.1.6 A Practical Technique: Defining Contributions, Responsibilities and Accountabilities

For teams whose members meet face to face for most of their working time the concepts of contribution, accountability and responsibility are mostly settled spontaneously. The team members have to cope with the underlying conflicts, because they are forced to continue to work with each other. For higher process levels it may happen that the persons contributing to the output of the processes only meet each other from time to time. Contributions, responsibilities and accountabilities have to be made more explicit and need some formalization. The method I use in this case I call *interface negotiations.* In contrast to classical forms of job descriptions, the outcome of an interface negotiation focuses upon interdependences between the team members and frees them to make their contributions in whatever way they wish:

(1) The members of a team define the outcomes for which they need one another: the outputs of the processes and their attributes which they want to stress. The list should not be longer than nine outputs, which already implies a common choice.
(2) Each of the team members answers individually the following questions:
   - What is your major contribution to the outcome of the team activities? Also, this is expressed more in terms of outcome than of activity.
   - What do I need as a contribution from each of the other team members to be able to realize my contribution successfully?
(3) The answers to the questions are shared and a discussion is started to settle the following issues :
   - If two or more members of the team think that they have to make the same contribution, overlap occurs. Somewhere there is a need for minimizing this to improve the efficiency of the team.
   - It may happen that one team member expects a contribution from someone who has not been mentioned by him or her. In this case this contribution must be given to someone. An organizational 'hole' has been discovered.
(4) The results of the negotiation are formally put in writing and form what may be called a management contract. This contract is the result of a strategic information process (Section 2.2.1) and contains the elements for the control (Section 2.2.2) of the outcome, for which the team is responsible or accountable. Reviewing how the contract has worked out during a certain period can start an audit information process (Section 2.2.3).

I used the interface negotiation to settle the relation between the regional divisions and the central services of a distribution company. Indicators were assigned to the several contributions and were the basis of a management information system. The negotiation was a forum in which the strategic choices of the whole company could be translated operationally. I use interface negotiations extensively when multidisciplinary product development groups are scattered over the research premises.

2.1.7 Clients, Actors, Owners: the Major Stakeholders of the Process

People in and around a process can have three major roles, which were defined by Checkland.

> *Those who contribute to the realization of the output of the process are assuming the actor's role. Those who are the beneficiaries or the victims of the output of the process are adopting the client's role. Those who can effectively decide to stop the process are assuming the owner's role.*

Although this part of the framework already refers to the interface between people and activities, it is worth thinking about these roles when defining a process. In any case, the people in the three roles must be involved in the definition of the processes and must agree on it. Remember that a definition is a decision and coming to a shared definition is also a decision process. Only when this shared definition exists can the negotiation around the needed contributions be fruitful. The stakeholders of that process are determined by the roles defined by Checkland.[3]

Beware of processes for which the three roles are taken by the same people: the probability is high that they will start to behave as a closed system. Many specialist staff functions or overspecialized work systems tend to become self-centred. From university faculties to large parts of the arms industry and the army, from therapy communities to computer departments, from governmental agencies to professional bodies, I have met the actor–owner–client collusion. Like all closed systems, these work systems are in danger of collapsing. In many cases they generate sickness in the people involved. Humans and social systems, like all living beings, need interactions with an outside world, an environment, to be able to develop the essential condition for survival.

When a public library is seen as a work system for keeping books in an orderly way, the librarians assume the roles of clients, actors and owners. All visitors are seen as disrupting this work system: they may damage books and create disorder by removing them from the shelves.

2.1.8 Environmental Constraints and *Weltanschauung*

Defining a work system through one or more processes is drawing boundaries. We define what does and does not belong to the processes, which activities and roles can be seen as contributing to them and which not. Every definition has to be placed in a context.

A dictionary has to give small phrases to enable the user to make a choice of possible translations. In Dutch, 'kost' means cost as well as food. It was rather an amusing experience when, in Croatia, I used the Croatian word for food, 'hrana', for costs. My pocket dictionary let me down there.

For this reason, Checkland has added two contextual elements to the definition of a process.

> *Environmental constraints are boundaries which are taken as immutable. They cannot be influenced but nevertheless are worth mentioning.*

They may refer to the walls of a building as well as to laws and regulations.

> Weltanschauung *is the implicit perspective which makes the definition of a process meaningful for the various parties involved.*

If a process is strongly tied to a business definition, its *Weltanschauung* implies that doing business is a worthwhile activity. If it relates to financial transactions, the implicit *Weltanschauung* is that money exchange is a better way of regulating business transactions than barter.

Again, the *Weltanschauung* refers to the stance, the perspective which different persons take for defining a work system: making the *Weltanschauung* explicit makes apparent the political nature of defining a work system. By political nature, I mean dealing with the different value systems that people have when they are involved in joint activities. *Weltanschauung* becomes a real issue when it is very difficult to find a consensus around the definition of a process.

A classical example has been given by Checkland.[3] While he was working for the Home Office in the UK, helping to develop a management information system for a prison, he found rather contradictory *Weltanschauungs*. A prison could be seen as a system to implement the punishments of the courts, to rehabilitate the inmates, for containing potential riots, an educational system for making more successful crooks, a system for keeping asocial people out of normal society. Eventually, a compromise was found between the different *Weltanschauungs* by defining a prison as a kind of hotel, hospital or boarding school: a system which admits people for a certain period of time and then discharges them.

2.1.9 The Management Process

In this framework, management is neither a position nor a function. It is a contribution from everyone who has an actor's role in a process.

> *Management consists of those contributions which transform the transactions of a process with its environment into a coherent pattern so that all the parties involved in the process— actors, clients and owners—are enabled to identify that process, its purpose and the development of its purpose. Management essentially is about meaning.*

Because only human beings are meaning processors, management processes have to be fulfilled by people. Conversely, if there is no management contribution for a human being in a work system, i.e. if there is no discretionary power to make a decision about what fits the process or what does not, then it is more humane to automate that task as soon as possible. In any case, every human being will attribute meaning to what he or she does and to what the others are doing and will take discretionary decisions. And he or she will behave accordingly: i.e. manages. Nevertheless, this does not mean that the output of the process always forms a coherent pattern. Once coherence disappears, the work system is at risk. Conversely, if the work system is working, i.e. it is able to create the output of its processes, coherence is somehow present. But for an observer, incoherence may result from the fact that the overt statement of the purpose of a work system differs from its implicit and covert purpose, which retains its coherence.

The driver of a lorry of ready-mixed concrete has no access to a building site. He has to take a decision about what to do, an autonomous decision. This is his contribution to a management process. Even if he telephones the dispatcher to ask him what to do, this decision is essential for the subsequent performance of the work system in which he is an actor. I have seen how, in strongly centrally controlled companies, he decides to drive his load back, even if he knows that it will be wasted. This apparently irrational behaviour only shows that the work system is not governed by the delivery of concrete but only by the control of its people. Much 'irrational' organizational behaviour can be understood in terms of a work system, which is governed only by justifying what one has done instead of anticipating what one could do. Management is then the prerogative of managers. The clients of these work systems are its managers.

Open-plan offices bring people together in one room, although they may not need to work with each other. Quickly they start to deploy activities which are only related to the fact that they are together. Maintaining or destroying plants, organizing initiation rites for newcomers, even starting to play golf with waste paper and baskets are expressions of the meaning which they create. On the other hand, where togetherness is ergonomic at director and board level, where the various actors are interdependent for the decisions which they have to make, we see long corridors with closed doors and an army of secretaries, who behave as guardians. These directors may be highly trained in communication skills, but this will not necessarily enhance the quality of their shared meaning. Fortunately, long coffee breaks may overcome their poor ergonomic environments.

The concepts developed so far can help the reader to start to differentiate between what people in the work system say about its purpose and its implicit purpose, which maintains coherence. The discipline needed to define the processes of a work system clarify its implicit coherence and incoherence.

Returning to our plant manager (Section 2.1.3), his telephone call to the supplier as a contribution to the first purchasing process can be assessed by the person accountable for that process. This person is entitled to evaluate the plant manager's contribution, whatever his organizational position. The object of the evaluation is the impact of the manager's telephone call upon the coherence of the process.

Once this mechanism is understood, performance appraisals change completely in nature. Bottom-up or top-down loses meaning once the process vocabulary is used. Performance appraisals can be seen as mutual evaluations of contributions to a shared output.

I have elaborated on the management process because most management problems can be exposed once these principles are understood. Managers can become less anxious when they no longer have the illusion that they are in charge of processes, while missing the opportunity to make active contributions to them, and when they become aware that they do not have to fulfil the expectations of their subordinates to keep up the image of being in charge. This applies as much for the President of the United States as for a gardener in the White House.

2.1.10 A Practical Example: Solving a Management-Succession Problem Using the Previous Concepts

I was once asked to help an agency in the difficult task of finding a successor to its charismatic and entrepreneurial leader, B. The fact that B himself asked for help was an indication of the nature of the problem and of his qualities. The success of the agency on two dimensions, the achievement of its aims as a pressure group and its financial soundness, were attributed mostly to B's leadership. His style of managing was very political indeed, but was accepted because as a person his integrity and devotion to the agency's aims were accepted by all parties involved, even by his adversaries.

The first message I tried to convey to the people working closest to B, a kind of co-ordination committee within the agency and part of the board of directors, called 'the office', was the fact that he was indeed irreplaceable. Literally, there was only one B. For the same reason, I started immediately to discuss the difficulty of the process in which they were involved. The mourning process of losing a 'great' leader would surely interfere with the choice of his successor.

Next, I gave the following task separately to the co-ordination committee and the office, between which B was the link: write down a list of the reasons for the existence of your group in terms of its services and products, its beneficiaries and the qualities people expect from those products and services, for whose realization you need one another. Leader B contributed to both lists. In fact I forced them to think about the meaning of the interdependencies between the group members to try to free them from their leadership obsession. They had to work hard on the task, because it changed completely the way they viewed the succession problem.

Later, I brought the two groups together with the lists they had made. Instead of a list of activities of the leader, which in a normal procedure would generate a profile impossible to match, I focused the persons working with B on why they were together, not on what they did or how they did it. The final list of services provided by both groups was then presented to the potential successors.

A meeting was organized between the participants of both groups with B and with each candidate for the succession. The candidate went into discussion with the group about which contribution he or she liked most and was most able to provide. At the same time, it became apparent which actual contributions of B would not be taken over by the candidate and could be taken care of by other members of the group or eventually by newcomers. Leadership and management were starting to be redistributed in the succession procedure itself.

2.2. RELATIONS BETWEEN WORK SYSTEMS AND BETWEEN PROCESSES: INFORMATION PROCESSES

From the previous elements of our vocabulary, it can be inferred that a work system can be mapped as a system of interlinked processes. For tackling management and organizational issues, it is worth looking at the interaction between processes from the perspective of information. *Information is the raw material for creating and conveying meaning, thus for management.* Based on Beer's Viable Systems Model, I use three different kinds of information processes, each with its own purpose (Figure 2.2).

2.2.1 Strategic Information Processes

All information processes which contribute to management, we call strategic information processes. These create, convey and develop meaning to all people involved in a work system.

Reality is immensely rich, hence it is unpredictable and intractable. People involved in activities continually have large or small decisions to take when they are confronted with the inescapable surprises that come from their transactions with that reality. When contributing to the same process, the many discretionary decisions they take must have a minimum of coherence. Otherwise the process loses its integrity. The information which enables people to take decisions independently in a coherent way is strategic information. The world view behind this statement says *that*

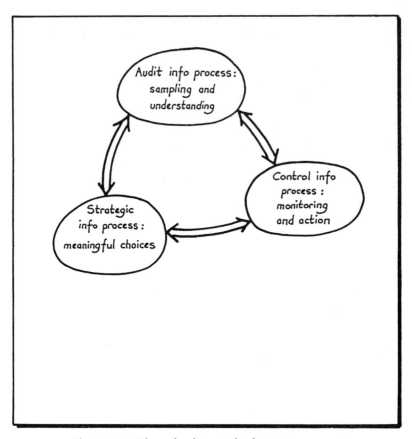

Figure 2.2 Three fundamental information processes

coherence in action is directly related to coherence in the meaning attributed to these actions.

The term 'strategic information processes' is a compromise. Since the beginning of the 1960's 'strategy' has become part of normal organizational jargon. Its military background has been forgotten. What are called strategic activities in organizations have, in my experience, much to do with the process I have defined. Strategic repositioning is still too often used as an excuse for creating victims, with the competition, the 'as if' enemy, as the main reason for it. I would have liked to use another term for strategic information processes, but this could make it more difficult to link the processes I describe with everyday managerial practice.

Let us take again the first process definition of our purchasing work system. The plant manager telephones the supplier because there is an urgent need for material.

The supplier replies that his accountant has blocked delivery because of a late payment. Somewhere in the process different perspectives have dictated small decisions, which now create a problem. Either this problem will become recurrent or the various parties must match their perspectives to improve the process. The way this matching is achieved is by what I call a 'strategic information process'. Manager and supplier may agree that when the debt is below a certain level, well-defined goods will be dispatched. The supplier's and manager's objectives lead to a meaningful procedure, taking into account the strategic interests of both.

One simple way to make people aware of this process is by having regular meetings between the major actors to discuss past individual decisions which they found relevant to that process, and to help each other to detect the implicit priorities each has used. After they have made an inventory of these priorities they can start to debate how these can be minimally matched. This whole set-up becomes a platform for strategic information processes.

Ideally, strategic information processes lead to a shared meaning about the processes to be managed among the people managing them. Debate between people and the dialectics between their perspectives is the only form of strategic information process. If contradiction and dissension cease between the people in a work system, it is then doomed to failure and usually creates victims when it fails.

The events in Eastern Europe, yesterday and today, as well as the loyalty ideology of high-involvement organizations in the West are indicative of a lack of effective strategic information processes. There is a paradox in the fact that if a work system is managed by 'yes-men' only, its coherence is at stake. This paradox is easily solved once the empirical fact is taken seriously that each human being is partly autonomous in his or her intentions and that the fusion of these intentions in a collective intention is an illusion or a self-delusion. The belief in that illusion leads to pathological group behaviour, as Bion has already pointed out in his Experiences in Groups.[4] 'Pathological' here means non-adapted to its environment.

A consequence of the definition of strategic information processes is that only actors have a role in them. In management literature, strategy has been reified. By distinguishing the object of a strategy from its subjects, we have already created an implementation problem. Strategy is not a product of top-down propaganda but an ongoing process at each process level of an organization. The interaction between work systems and their environment is the locus of these processes. Strategies which are perceived as pure cerebral activities, as products of management think tanks and which result from conclaves which define 'stars' and 'cows' and 'dogs' will never be more than dreams. Dreams are the beautiful result of cerebral processes, which have shut out completely the input of the senses. Dreams do not need eyes, ears, noses, mouths, hands and feet.

When I am asked to accompany management teams in sorting out what they call their strategy, I use three dimensions. First, I focus them much more upon discovering how their company relates to their major stakeholders than to their competition. Second, I permit them to have their individual dreams, to define their company based on their different *Weltanschauungs*. Third, I urge them to translate the results of their debates into a communication plan throughout their company and to permit the translation of the meaning they discovered in its endeavours into the primary processes, i.e. the processes which express physically the purpose of the company to its customers.

2.2.2 Control Information Processes

Control information processes are those which lead to a corrective, regulative action by the people contributing to transformation processes. Control information flows through a corrective feedback loop (Figure 2.3).

There is a minimum number of features necessary to permit control processes. First, the transformation processes to be controlled must be permanently monitored for relevant events. The strategic information processes clarify what can be seen as relevant or not: nevertheless, the choice of relevant events always implies a risk. We may choose to monitor the wrong events. Good strategic information is a necessary but not sufficient condition for good control processes. Due to the surprises of reality, no control process can be perfect: we have to live with the existential risk of breakdowns. Usually the complexity of control systems is a result of the negation of that risk. This makes them very expensive and dangerous because of the false expectation they create that one can be completely in control.

When I ask in bureaucratic organizations which performance indicators are used, I often receive lists of 30 or more. In one instance there was a monthly report with about 500 indicators. In practice, people use around seven indicators. The costs of measuring and working with a very large number of performance indicators are hidden in the budgets for information technology, one of the managerial sacred cows.

Next, the result of our monitoring must be compared with a desired output. Control only has meaning when we act to diminish any discrepancy between what we want and what happens. For this reason, we should

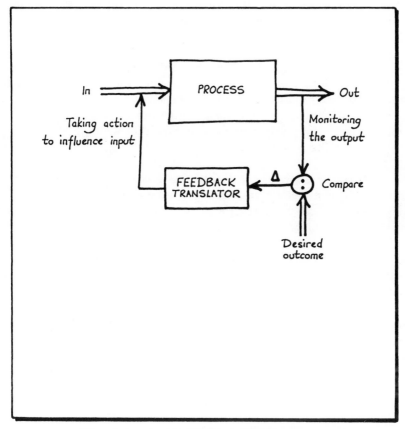

Figure 2.3   Control or corrective feedback process

avoid information overload in the people empowered to take control action by filtering out the monitoring data which do not show a discrepancy. *Control information processes provide information by exception.* Subsequently, all indicators which lack one or more norms are useless for controlling purposes.

As the basic purpose of control information processes is to steer, its form should be as simple as possible. There is no need to explain why discrepancies occur. The implicit understanding of the processes to be regulated by the one who steers makes the action relevant or not.

Our plant manager has a warning of an imminent material shortage: he need not inquire why this happened, he only requires the right reflex to pick up his telephone and ring the supplier. The implicit strategic information is that shortages of material are essentially bad, and thus to be corrected. The implicit or explicit norm is zero shortages.

In my experience there are three major reasons why control systems of this kind are underdeveloped in most organizations, other than in the domain of their primary processes:

• The first relates directly to defective strategic information processes.
• The second is that the implicit norm in bureaucratic organizations is that errors, deviations, discrepancies in themselves are bad things. Instead of control action, this attitude generates justification action: for this reason, much effort is put into explaining after the event why the discrepancy occurred, or who has been guilty of it, instead of quick corrective action.
• The third reason is much more pernicious. It confuses a sense of responsibility for others with a prerogative to take control action. Control is delegated upwards to those persons who do not participate in the processes to be controlled.

All work systems are essentially self-regulated. External controls are mythical features which cost large amounts of money and frustration and, furthermore, are completely inadequate. He who thinks he is controlling from without is asking to be cheated by those whom he thinks he controls. Controller and controlled alike are colluding in this lie. This applies as much to the President of the United States as to a gardener in the White House. Once existential risks are accepted and the anxiety about things getting out of control is reduced to a realistic dimension, control information processes are very easy to design and implement. Moreover, they become much simpler, hence cheaper.

When people are 'cooking the books', it does not always mean that they are doing harm. It is their way of coping with the surprises of the reality which they must confront in contrast to all kinds of 'shoulds' and 'should nots'. It is their way of self-regulating, thus surviving under ever-changing circumstances. When planning objectives are imposed, they will either be met on paper or the external environment will be invoked to justify failing to meet them. Both sides, the controller and the controlled, know this and in this way irresponsibility becomes institutionalized.

2.2.3 Information Processes for Understanding the Work System or Audit Information Processes

Suppose that our plant manager has made four urgent telephone calls to the same supplier in one month. If he has any time left, he starts to reflect. Something must be systematically wrong in the way the process for meeting the needs for material is effected. While he is telephoning he thinks he is doing the right thing, but afterwards, while reflecting, he asks himself if the right thing is also the best. He is starting to develop an audit information process.

Audit information processes are those which lead the actors to a more profound understanding of why the process is carried out, what it does, with what means it is performed and how these means are used.

While control information processes lead to action, audit information processes result in understanding. While control information processes require a participative stance, audit information processes need an observer stance. Exactly for this reason, *audit information processes belong to the next higher process level than the process being audited.* Understanding requires a certain degree of detachment from the process itself. Audit information processes can ask questions about the finality of the process itself and the way it is performed relative to its purpose. This is impossible while steering: the course cannot be questioned at that time, otherwise corrective action is impossible since deviations from the course lose their meaning.

Audit processes can use four sources of data. Audit processes are usually started when something is going wrong, when breakdowns occur in the work system and its processes. This kind of process we call *ad-hoc problem diagnosis.* It may happen that, for security and prevention reasons, potential problem diagnosis is made with a fixed frequency, once a month, once a year, etc. This we call *potential problem diagnosis.* But diagnosis does not necessarily have to focus upon problems. It may be worth investigating and understanding why the process is working and how it delivers its output to the satisfaction of its clients. This kind of diagnosis creates positive energy and leads more easily to improvements than does the focus upon sickness and problems. I like to call these audit processes *ad hoc and potential system diagnosis.*

Our plant manager can be helped to understand the problems with his one supplier in a way which leads to improvement action when he has a good insight into how the process works well for all his other suppliers. If the system is able to do a good job for certain suppliers, then the mechanisms which are already in place can, by analogy, be used to deal with the problematic supply.

The fashion of organizational benchmarking, in which one organization compares its operations to those of a competitor or to an organization with similar operations, can be seen as a system diagnosis.

This is a much easier and cheaper task than to invent and implement a whole new process. Many painful experiences of system changes generated by problem diagnosis could have been initially avoided by a good system diagnosis.

It is self-evident that control and audit information processes are a rich source for strategic information processes. *Part of the data used for audit information on one process level can be used as data for control information on the next higher process level.*

The data of a time series of a machine's process parameter can show a systematic oscillation (Figure 2.4). This is caused by a control action which changes the set-up of the process. Analysis of the time series results in an understanding of the wearing pattern of a certain tool. This may lead to monitoring the tool so that its replacement, a different control action, is carried out at the right time. The audit information has made control action on the lowest process level superfluous. The same process parameter has been used for first controlling the machine operation, then for understanding the process behaviour and for implementing a control system on the next higher process level.

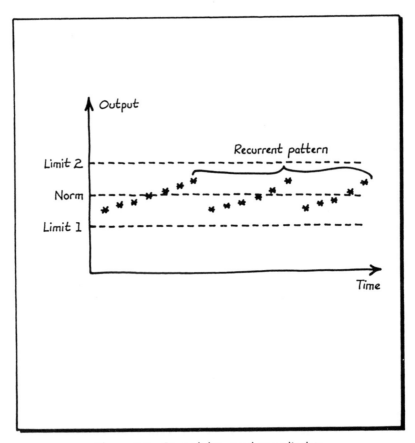

Figure 2.4   Control data used as audit data

For the various actors, owners and clients of the process, both control and audit information provide the common experiential raw material on which to debate the meaning of their work. In many cases the three processes are easily concurrent with each other. When breakdowns occur in the information and communication processes it may be useful to consider the work system through the definitions, given by our concepts. But it is also an interesting exercise to spot the three different information processes in healthy work systems.

The maintenance record of an electricity generator deteriorated from a certain point in time. An *ad hoc* problem analysis showed that this coincided with the removal of a coffee machine, due to a costcutting exercise. The coffee machine was the place where the electrical and the mechanical maintenance engineers met to discuss joint control action. As electrical and mechanical maintenance belonged to two different departments, this was the only place where it could be planned. A system analysis using the concepts of process level and control information would have made the parties aware of the role of this meeting place.

2.3 PROCESS LEVELS AND TIME SPAN

If thinking in process levels is a normal human way to create order out of the complexity of intertwined activities and contributions, can it be that, in the way we think as human beings, some ordering principle works? Elliott Jaques, after 40 years of research, has answered this question affirmatively. As the only measure for this ordering principle he uses *time span: i.e. the time needed to materialize the results of activities deployed.* The longer the time span, the higher the process level. Let us return to our purchasing work system.

The planning of a good customer–supplier contract to create the conditions for just-in-time delivery of materials will take longer than the deliveries themselves. Procedures have to be designed, and plans made and tested which will eventually lead to a workable supply that meets the requirements for customer and supplier alike. But starting such a relation with a supplier must be embedded in a longer-term policy which justifies the effort to make such a contract. The relevance of this policy cannot be seen in isolation from the development of the whole business and the demands which the market and the competition will make in the years to come.

Elliott Jaques has been able to define a classification of time spans, which are linked with the capacity of human beings to work with definite time spans. He calls this 'work capacity' and he has classified it into what he calls 'strata'. Each stratum has its own task complexity and time span. In the next chapter I will make extensive use of the different strata, discovered by Jaques, to make a typology of processes and process levels.

2.4 SPAN OF RELATIONS AS A CONSTRAINT ON SIZE OF WORK SYSTEMS

As a final basic concept I wish to introduce a bold conjecture related to the size of work systems. If work systems can be seen as the combination of a system of activities and a system of relations, and if relations can never be defined as anonymous, then there is a maximum number of actors, clients and owners which can be included in the network of relations. Instead of the classical concept of span of control, I introduce the concept of 'span of relations'. *The span of relations is the maximum number of people able to attribute a shared meaning to the system of relations they develop through the system of activities in which they are involved.*

Before quantifying the span of relations it is necessary to elaborate on the world view behind this definition:

- Many of the problems with which 'big' organizations are confronted are generated by an implicit assumption which reifies them. This assumption is that the organization is best defined as an aggregate of people.

    We speak of IBM having 300 000 employees and firing 50 000 of them. What this means in terms of relations is ignored. Markets are seen as aggregates of real and potential customers. The major part of economic theory only recognizes aggregates, aggregated preferences, aggregated needs and aggregated offer and demand. The relational aspects of economic behaviour are also mostly ignored.

    The physical metaphor which is the most relevant for describing aggregates is the theory of gases. The behaviour of the aggregate can be described for gases because each molecule in a gas has a minimum set of interactions (collisions) with other molecules. When these interactions become bonds (more or less fixed relations as in liquids and solids) non-linear behaviour becomes normal and other characteristics emerge.

- The assumption at the basis of the concepts I am developing uses a systemic metaphor. I look at 'big' organizations as networks of work systems, which are more or less loosely coupled. This coupling is not made through invisible or anonymous mechanisms but through people who, consciously or unconsciously, are adopting various roles in differing work systems.

    Even markets are not aggregates of individual molecules looking for a linear balance between supply and demand. Relations between the market makers influence strongly how they rank their individual preferences and how they construct the non-linear fluctuating price. The behaviour of the stock exchange, the basic metaphor for market forces, is better described by chaos theory and self-regulated, strongly coupled, non-linear systems theory than by linear equations and equilibria.

- A logical step further is to consider the informational transactions between the various related actors as the basis for the creation, the maintenance and the development of a shared meaning. These are transactions between real people, who know each other personally in some way or other. Although they may be immersed in data, these data only influence collective behaviour when they are processed by living networks.

Everyone has noticed the strong impact of rumours on collective behaviour. Organizational theorists have inadvertently coined the concept of informal organization to point to the most important informational part of organizational life. Social constructivists have pointed out that organizational and economic behaviour is best seen as the result of dialogues between many parties. The enunciation of sociological or economical laws leads to self-fulfilling prophecies. When, as a consultant, I am called in to deal with a certain kind of problem I begin to hear everyone interpreting events in terms of the assumed problem. Barbara Czarniawska-Jörges[5], of the University of Lund, illustrates this in her study of the relation between consultants and their client organizations. She illustrates how the consultant's discourse interacts with the perception of the problem by the client.

Very little research has been done on the span of relations. I have to refer here to some small group research which started with Homans just before the Second World War and which was continued by the Tavistock Institute in London and the National Training Laboratory in the United States after the war. When I give some indications on the width of the span of relations, I use their findings but I also rely heavily on my own experience of working with groups and organizational units of quite different sizes.

For the kind of result that a group of people can achieve and the necessary development of their personal relation I discovered three kinds of social systems.

2.4.1 The Small Group : with a Maximum of about Nine People: The Creative Group

Only members of small groups can create or discover something new and share their commitment to nurture what they have brought to fruition. Difficult decisions, which require strong commitment from the whole decision-making body, are always taken by such groups, although sometimes the formal responsibility for the decision rests upon a larger body.

A Non-Governmental Organization (NGO), involved in Third World development in the North, asked me to help them with the succession of their charismatic leader. Formally, the decision-making body consisted of the General Council, represented by a board of 25 people. Each was the representative of a local NGO. Immediately, I started to inquire how decisions were really made. A small group of the board, informally called the Office and consisting of six members of the board, was indicated as the 'real' decision-making body.

It is clear that I refer here to decisions as creative acts, involving risks for the decision makers. In organizational literature many so-called decisions do not fulfil this requirement. If they do, I invite the reader to look for the decision-making body as a small group, whatever the formal statements about the way in which decisions are taken: whether by voting, by an algorithm, or by a representative body. This statement is also valid for political decision-making bodies. When I see large conferences being assumed to take decisions I try to deduce where the real decision-making power is, or whether the conference is structurally unable to make any decision.

2.4.2 The Large Group with a Maximum of about 80 People: The Reflective Group

The members of these groups are able to debate jointly the shared meaning of the activities in which they are involved and their desired outcomes. For these debates they can form either small creative subgroups or they can constitute sounding boards for the creative subgroups. Large groups can work either as project groups or as political platforms.

Entrepreneurial groups as instituted by BSO in Holland, by Kyocera in Japan or by Bata all over the world before the Second World War are typical examples of the use of the capabilities of large groups. They are able to materialize a shared vision. The cell structure which these companies use is limited to 30 to 50 people. They form strong social systems.

Another example is given by many sports groups or by the basic battle unit in armies.

Work units which are designed on socio-technical principles are also limited to about 50 people.

Project groups in Research & Development environments start to get into trouble once they become larger than 50 to 60 people.

Referent organizations, search conferences or working representative bodies are also limited to about 80 people. These are groups which must be able to come to a consensus. By consensus I mean that no-one in the group vetos the outcome, which is communicated to the outside world by the group. This is quite different from unanimity, where every member is strongly committed to the outcome. Advisory boards or groups of representatives of different world views are best limited to a large group. Intensive personal interactions and debate, necessary to arrive at acceptance of the outcomes, put a constraint upon the number of people involved.

The difficulties in the EC when they move from a group of six to a group of 12 and even more can be analysed from this perspective. It is clear that in a group of six the group loses its efficiency when coalitions are starting to form within the group, while in a group of 12, coalitions are unavoidable and are even necessary to reach a consensus. The fact that every member can change coalition for different issues leads to a spirit of compromise. And good compromises, based upon consensus, are the best that can be achieved in large groups.

I call large groups 'reflective groups' because their members can start to reflect upon what the group is doing without feeling the pressure of their peers to be completely involved. At the same time, some members are working, while others are observing and reflecting. The level of energy spent by different members in working and reflecting can also vary widely, without the pressure to be equally involved, which is typical of small groups. Even a certain level of absenteeism does not disrupt large groups. In small groups absenteeism strongly disables the group: the presence of the absent member is felt as a weight.

2.4.3 The Adaptive Group with a Maximum of about 700 People

Small enterprises seem to have difficulty in developing, once they pass a certain threshold in the number of their employees. There is a need to start to operate in a different way: what has been done previously (usually informally), the experience that has developed in each employee, the mutual adaptation which takes place continuously with changes in and outside the company, can no longer be dealt with in the same way. A need for formalization, specialization and differentiation is felt. The enterprise shifts its *modus operandi*. From a whole work system, which shows a certain degree of adaptability, it becomes a network of different work systems, which have to formalize their interdependencies into more explicit contracts. Not everyone knows everyone else. Not everyone deals with the others. Flexibility and adaptability are lost. The concept of a work system as a system of activities and relations breaks down.

We can no longer speak of one work system. I have not found any research on the maximum span of relations which we can define as one work system. A maximum of 700 is based upon the answer given by myself and colleagues on how many persons we can remember: 700 is exceptionally high, 200 is more a median. Thus it becomes meaningless to speak of larger entities as if they were monolithic work systems or organizations. We only can define larger entities as aggregates, anonymous classifications, which are social constructs but not relevant in terms of interventions and improvement.

My claim is that for those activities which are directed towards the improvement of our human condition, the concept of a social system reduces to that of a work system, characterized by a physiological constraint: the span of relations. This has an important consequence for the relevance of sociological, political and organizational generative theories and their practice. It permits me in my work as a practitioner to focus upon the right number and to work within feasible boundaries.

When a managing director or a chief executive officer of a large company asks me to help her to improve 'her' organization I know that she means the total organization or corporation. But I focus her attention on the work systems to which she is personally contributing, on her major stakeholders, who have to be given their proper names, as persons, not as entities. And slowly she realizes that by improving those work systems and their interfaces with other semi-autonomous work systems we are in fact dealing with the issue at hand, even if initially it was given one large label: an organizational issue.

Similarly, I try to contribute to 'organizational restructuring'. It is sufficient to review and improve the functioning of three process levels and their interfaces with neighbouring work systems to make the necessary adaptations by redistributing relevant tasks. Once one is trapped in the monolithic hierarchical model of the whole organization, the exercise becomes futile, and leads to a very wasteful process. In most practical cases, the number of people involved is less than 200.

The Mondragon Co-operative Experience in the Basque country, which has about 22 000 members at present, has organically developed into about 100 semi-autonomous co-operatives and the decentralization of ABB (Asea-Brown Boveri) into quasi-autonomous business units follows more or less the same principle.

It is not my aim to attack frontally the whole body of knowledge built around the concepts of social systems, in which apparently the number of people and their interrelations is not specified. The concepts of a country, a corporation, a market, a target group like women, or the unemployed are not erroneous in themselves. They may be used legitimately in all kinds of debate or discourse, even scientific ones. I only look at social systems as a practitioner whose primary aim is to improve human affairs. For this endeavour, the concept of work system , with its limited span of relations, is the most relevant. Small is not always beautiful, but 'big' is always a delusion when it refers to organizational action. This delusion may be seen as the source of the self-defeating arrogance of power and its intrinsic corruption.

As the concept of span of relations is central to my view on work systems, I invite the practising reader to review his or her experience of improving work systems using the framework which I provide. If light can be shed upon the successes and failures in endeavours by using the framework, then for me this is sufficient empirical evidence of its relevance. For those who like to ground their scepticism upon 'harder' arguments I can only refer to the following items of theory:

(1) Miller[6] has pointed out that our brain is able to process seven plus or minus two parameters and their relations at the same time. It is not therefore surprising that small intensive groups are composed of a maximum of seven plus or minus two members.

(2) I mentioned previously that normal human beings are able to work on three process levels at the same time. This means that we may expect emergent characteristics to appear for groups with about $7 \times 7 = 49$

members and 7 ×7 ×7 = 343 members. Each member of the group of seven can perceive seven other members and their interrelations on the next two process levels. The tolerance of plus or minus two broadens the range to maximally 81 members for the reflective group and 729 for the adaptive one.

REFERENCES

1. Porter, M. (1980). *Competitive Strategy*, The Free Press
2. Beer, S. (1981). *The Brain of the Firm*, Wiley
3. Checkland, P. (1981). *Systems Thinking, Systems Practice*, Wiley
4. Bion, W. (1961). *Experiences in Groups*, Basic Books
5. Czarniawska-Jörges, B. (1988). *To Coin a Phrase*, Stockholm School of Economics
6. Miller, G.A. (1956). The magical number seven, plus or minus two: Some limits on our capacity for processing information, *Psychological Review*, **63**

Chapter 3

___ The Four Domains: Definition and General Characteristics

3.1 FIRST APPROACH

Although organizations are mostly described in the literature, as top–bottom anonymous hierarchical pyramids, and thus as monolithic entities, everyone who has experience of a work system is aware that he or she is dealing only with a limited number of people who occupy the actor, owner or client roles. Work systems are never anonymous. Anonymous sociological categories such as markets, classes, nations, the poor, the shareholders, etc. are ideological devices mostly used for justifying the unpleasant aspects of whatever contributions we are supposed to make.

A cashier in a distribution centre shapes his or her behaviour on real persons, bosses and supervisors, the regular customers, who, after a while, will be choosing his or her check-out, etc. In the same way, both a gardener in the White House and the President of the United States have their own networks of 'old boys' for or against whom they are working.

In practical work each of us is dealing with networks of living people, who are more or less distant from our concerns and the purpose we attribute to our activities. With these people we have our strategic debates. They are our allies, enemies, friends or adversaries, or a combination of them in different settings. They form the real network of relations in which we deploy our activities. They are partners in our work systems. Anonymous relations are a contradiction in terms. They are essentially platonic, thus ideological in nature. By ideological, I mean that they lead to unresolvable debates, because each party involved in the debate takes an ideological stance as if it were the only 'reality', which cannot be discussed. The terms of the debate are either/or, because the ideological *Weltanschauung* knows only 'the' reality.

Abstract relations cannot belong to real work only to symbolic actions. Activities can be done on an abstract level, but relations between people are never abstract.

The framework I want to develop now has as its aim to enable anyone to discover the work systems, the sets of relations and activities in which one is working and the different contributions one is making in this network. The purpose of the framework is to develop a model which is an alternative to bureaucratic anonymous ideological models. In a time when there is distrust of 'big machines', the theoretical institutions we have devised, headquarters, business units, governments, parties, agencies, Third World, etc., in a time when everyone is already regarding network organizations as the form for the future, there is a need for an adequate model to describe and prescribe this phenomenon.

The basic structure of the framework uses the work capacity strata, as defined by Elliott Jaques in his various works. I identify *one process level with one stratum*. As communications can be meaningfully made between three process levels, thus between three strata, I define *four domains, each containing three successive strata*.

The first domain I call the *added-value domain*. It consists of activities ranging from stratum 1 to stratum 3 in Jaques's term. This means that *its activities encompass a time span from 1 day to 2 years*. The second domain is the *innovation domain*. It consists of activities from stratum 3 to stratum 5 in Jaques's terms, and means that *its activities encompass a time span from 1 to 10 years*. The reader will have noticed that stratum 3, with a time span between 1 and 2 years, may belong to two domains. The simple reason is that relations between two domains need an overlapping set of common activities. Between the added-value and the innovation domain, these are activities belonging to stratum 3. The third domain is the *value-systems domain*. It consists of activities ranging from stratum 5 to stratum 7 in Jaques's terms, and means that *its activities encompass a time span from 5 to 50 years*. Here again, stratum 5, which contains activities from 5 to 10 years, forms a hinge between the innovation and the value-system domain. The fourth domain is *the spiritual domain*. It consists of *activities with a time span greater than 20 years* (see Figure 3.1).

Each of the domains has its own emergent characteristics. In fact, the output of the work systems operating in a 'higher' domain are creating the conditions for the underlying domain. I want to make it very clear that, in contrast to a certain interpretation of Jaques's work, a higher domain does not manage the activities of a lower one, or that activities of a higher domain only can express themselves in terms of abstractions.

In systemic thinking the environment of a system always refers to a higher conditioning level. In Ashby's terms, the variety of the environment of a system is greater than the variety of the system itself. This does not mean that the environment is completely determining the system. Maturana and Varela[1] have correctly pointed out the autopoietic characteristics of all living systems. Their interactions with their environment show a great degree of autonomy, because of the selective way in which these systems perceive and act upon their environment.

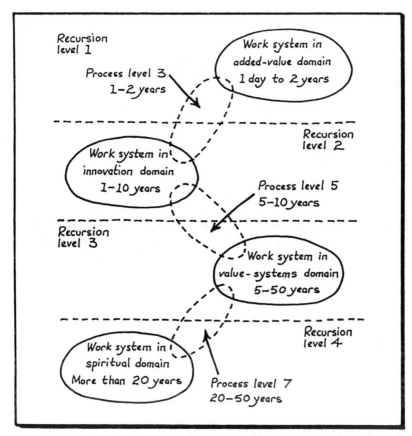

Figure 3.1 Overview of the four domains and their time spans

In less theoretic terms: the soil, the weather and their mutual interaction can be seen as conditions for the growth and development of the various species in an area. They provide necessary but not sufficient conditions. Even the interactions of the individual species with their environment can create effects upon that environment. Allen[2] shows how the species in an ecological system may produce terpenes, which heighten the probability of a wood fire and thus create very specific climatic conditions for the biotope itself.

The best way in which I can clarify the relation between the various domains is by the story of the four stonemasons.

3.2 THE STORY OF THE FOUR STONEMASONS

During my travels I came to a city and saw on its outskirts great works being undertaken by many stonemasons. I started to inquire what was happening and asked one: 'What are you doing?' He answered: 'I am cutting my 20 stones a day, so that in the evening

I can go home with my daily wage and am able to feed, clothe and shelter my wife and children.' I went to a second stonemason and again asked what he was doing. He answered: 'I am struggling with a new chisel that I designed last week. Some of the stones cannot be cut because of their difficult grain. I don't like to throw them away and am looking to cut them beautifully against that grain. I have nearly succeeded in making the right chisel: four of my previous attempts have failed, but I have the feeling that now I am succeeding.' I went to a third stonemason and again asked what he was doing. He answered: 'Look around you! Don't you see that I am building a cathedral?' Much impressed, I went to a fourth stonemason and asked what he was doing. He turned his head towards me, looked me straight in the eyes and said: 'Don't you see that I am cutting stones?' After that I stopped travelling and lived in that city, because it was a good place to stay.

I would like to make several points here:

(1) You have probably realized that the four stonemasons are examples of the four domains. The first belongs to the added-value domain, the second to the innovation domain, the third to the value-systems domain and the fourth to the spiritual domain.

(2) To be able to locate in which domain a person is making contributions, one cannot rely upon his or her behaviour. Only communication permits us to grasp the perspective or the domain in which he or she is working. More precisely, doers do not necessarily work within the lowest domain nor thinkers within the highest. When we come to the description of typical activities of the spiritual domain, we will be confronted with the fact that these have mostly a very physical expression. I want to stress that point, because Elliott Jaques's concepts are often misinterpreted as a justification for a meritocratic class society, in which the abstract and complex thinkers are seen to have the 'right' to manage or even direct the others.

(3) Every domain has its own emergent characteristics which cannot be deduced from the others. The language of each domain and its interests are quite different. Hence the need of an overlapping stratum. There is thus no hierarchical power relation between the activity domains. Designing them as hierarchical management levels is not very helpful, either in the understanding of their meaning, or in improvement efforts. The 'Requisite Organization' of Elliott Jaques[3] is in fact a book which prevents the fruitful use of his ideas and discoveries.

3.3 RELATING RECURSION LEVELS WITH THE DOMAINS

One of the basic concepts developed by Beer in his Viable Systems Model[4] is the concept of a recursion level. In its most elementary formulation the Recursive System Theorem is as follows.

In a recursive organizational structure any viable system contains and is contained in a viable system.

When looking up the many examples in Espejo and Harnden[5] it appeared that organizational formal boundaries are too easily taken for granted to define the different recursion levels. A 'pathological' approach towards these organizations leads to the detection of system failures relative to the five subsystems of a Viable System and their interrelations. Indeed, if there are so many pathologies in 'big' organizations, as indicated by the many examples given, then perhaps we are looking in a very biased way to what we take for viable systems. Our world of work seems to be able to adapt itself quite successfully to all kinds of calamities, sometimes due to natural causes but mostly caused by the 'human' factor. The resilience of human culture is much stronger than 'organizational pathologists' can explain. Instead of making lots of 'problem diagnosis' I prefer to start with what I call 'systems diagnosis'. Why is it that human affairs are so resilient, when, at the same time, we seem to be able to create such large 'messes'?

If in human endeavours the definition of a work system as a system of activities and relations is meaningful, then we can start to look at Viable Systems from quite a different perspective. I have tried to show previously how, in the human being, the elementary Viable System of human culture, work systems are meaning-forming devices which we use in our span of relations to improve and to develop. Jaques's concept of work capacity and time span as an individual property makes sense of how different people perceive their environments. And as social beings, they share within the constraints of their understanding of three strata or three process levels their images of organizations within the constraints of the span of relations.

Based upon these premises, I suggest, as a practitioner, to work with the four domains as the four recursion levels of all human affairs. I have mentioned earlier that each domain has its own emerging characteristics as a viable system. Each domain creates necessary but not sufficient conditions for the activities of a lower domain, but each is operating in a quasi-autonomous way in its own set of activities .

One of the oldest enterprises in Western Europe is the Italian wine producer and distributor Villa Antinori. It was founded in the fourteenth century and is still successfully operating. As we will see later, this kind of activity resorts to the added-value domain. It can be seen as a Viable System. During its history, Villa Antinori has not been an innovator in the way it makes, stores and distributes wine. Nevertheless, it has adopted all the oenological innovations as well as those in the storage, transport and sale of wine, so that it still remains viable. Thus, the next recursion level for Villa Antinori can be seen as those activities in the innovative domain which may have occurred everywhere and which have been assimilated by it. These innovations, from the works of Pasteur to the reshaping of the retail distribution systems, created conditions for the development of Villa Antinori. In no way has there been an organizational superstructure which enabled Villa Antinori to adopt these innovations. Even more, the innovative work systems, relevant to the wine business, were distributed over many sectors and over a long time. They can be analysed as a Viable Work System only through the approach of the span of relations, which permitted their assimilation by Villa Antinori. In its turn, the innovations I have referred to are embedded in the next recursion level: the value-systems domain. In this domain, for centuries, people interested in the cultural significance of wine have sponsored and stimulated conditions in which it was worth putting effort and money into the innovation of wine making, storage and distribution. Here again, only the lobbying and sponsoring groups can be seen as Viable Systems of the value-systems domain in relation to the innovators in the innovation domain. And these lobbyists and sponsors were inspired by the long-standing spiritual meaning of the making and the consumption of wine, so beautifully expressed in the Biblical figure of Noah: in our Western tradition, the discoverer of the eternal meaning of wine for human beings (Genesis).

I have developed this example to clarify certain aspects of the identification of recursion levels with the activity domains:

(1) The metaphor of a Russian doll that is used for explaining the recursion levels is rather misleading. Although one recursion level embeds another one, the emergent characteristics of one recursion level are quite different from those of the next, unlike Russian dolls. A better metaphor is to consider a cell as one viable system, embedded in an organism as a viable system at the next higher recursion level, or as one organism in a biotope embedded in this biotope. Later I will explain the consequences of this view for work systems: *organization structures are only meaningful devices in the added-value domain. In others they lose their meaning.*

(2) The relation between work systems of a higher domain with those of a lower one is not that of management and control. An organism is not managing or controlling a cell, it is creating conditions for its viability. In the same way, a biotope is not managing or controlling an organism but is creating conditions for its viability. Work systems in the innovation domain are not managing or controlling work systems in the added-value domain, they are only creating conditions for their viability. No oenological research management institute has managed Villa Antinori. In Chapter 8 I will give more details of the relation between the four activity domains and will consider the implications of seeing them as different recursion levels. But one can already start to think about the meaning of holdings and corporations, once their headquarters are seen not as being on a higher recursion level but at the same level as the divisions and business units they are supposed to manage. In the same way, one can ask whether innovations can be made inside work systems in the added-value domain. Finally, one can ask why states and governments, which theoretically belong to the value-systems domain, are organized in the same way as businesses.

3.4 STRUCTURE OF THE CHAPTERS ON EACH DOMAIN

In the next four chapters we will develop the characteristics of each domain and of the three strata or process levels belonging to it. Each chapter will contain:

(1) The generic transformation process of the work system of the domain.
(2) The emergent characteristics of the output of work systems belonging to the domain.
(3) A set of characteristics belonging to the three process levels or strata of the domain:
  (a) A generic description of the transformation process belonging to that stratum.
  (b) The basic strategic dilemma with which people working in that stratum are confronted. This is an indication of the content of the strategic debates belonging to that process level.
  (c) The general characteristics of the form and content of control and audit information processes belonging to the process level.
  (d) The general characteristics of development projects belonging to the process level.
(4) Examples of intervention techniques, which are relevant for improving the activities in the domain.

REFERENCES

1. Maturana, U. and Varela, F. (1980). *Autopoiesis and Cognition*, Reidel Publishing Company
2. Allen, T. and Starr, T. (1982). *Hierarchy, Perspectives for Ecological Complexity*, University of Chicago Press
3. Jaques, E. (1989). *The Requisite Organization*, Cason Hall
4. Beer, S. (1979). *The Heart of Enterprise*, Wiley
5. Espejo, R. and Harnden, R. (1990). *The Viable System Model, Interpretations and Applications of Stafford Beer's VSM*, Wiley

Chapter 4

The Added-value Domain: from a Time Span of 1 Day to one of 2 Years

4.1 BASIC DESCRIPTION OF THE DOMAIN

In section 2.1.3 I mentioned that most people can relevantly contribute to three process levels. For this reason, it is useful to group the process levels into domains: the domain of one work system on one recursion level (Figure 4.1). The purchasing work system example (Section 2.1.2) can be used as a reference. The domain which encompasses process levels 1 to 3, i.e. the time span of *1 day to 2 years*, we call the *added-value domain*. The basic process which belongs to this domain can be described as follows (Figure 4.1):

A set of relatively homogeneous requirements of a group of clients are transformed into those requirements being met so that clients, owners and actors can appreciate the relevance of the work system. In the added-value domain added and subtracted value is created for its clients, actors and owners alike.

Let us first look at this definition before we proceed to the description of the three process levels encompassed by this domain. I like to call this domain the added-value domain because it encompasses all human exchange activities between 'suppliers' and 'customers'. In this exchange, human care and creativity is expressed between the two parties and is appreciated as an added value by them. The basic reason of existence and hence the viability of these work systems resides in the mutual appreciation of the added value pertaining to this exchange. The added-value domain is the economic domain *par excellence.*

It is unimportant if the added value is defined financially in terms of profits or margins. The appreciation ultimately expresses itself in the maintenance of the supplier–customer relation, hence in the viability of its components: the supplier work system and the client work system. Supply and demand are not seen as abstract forces, regulating a market price, but as the systemic relation between two parties, who know each other and what they want. They rely upon each other for fulfilling their needs.

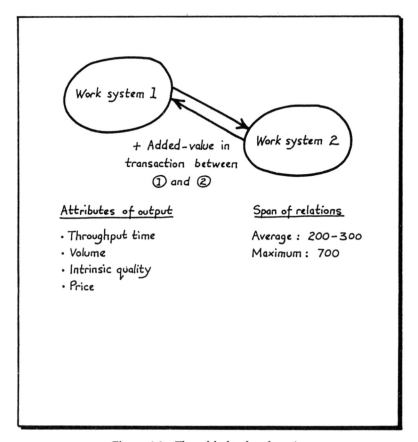

Figure 4.1   The added-value domain

These needs must have a certain degree of homogeneity. The work system cannot provide everything for everyone. Only those customers can be treated as kings for whom the capabilities of the supplier system match their requirements. To make this work system manageable for its clients, actors and owners alike, the range of requirements must be limited. These requirements can be expressed as four attributes of the output of the work system in the added-value domain.

4.1.1 Throughput Time

This is the time between the formulation of the requirement of the client until it is met to his or her satisfaction. A criterion for the homogeneity of the throughput time is evidently the time span required for the process. It should belong to one stratum.

In psychiatric hospitals it is a custom to have different wards for short-term patients and for what are called chronic patients: their nursing and treatment belong to different work systems.

Engineering departments and, more generally, specialist staff departments provide services, which mostly belong to different strata. Troubleshooting activities have different characteristics from improvement and development work. If a staff member is charged with these different tasks, he or she will place his or her priorities as a function of the time span with which they are most at ease. Moreover, many problems related to the management of staff departments can be more clearly understood, once it becomes clear that its activities do not belong to one work system, because of the range in throughput time.

If we link the concept of throughput time with the time span of a stratum we are able to ask some relevant questions about the way work is measured. The shortest time span in the added-value domain is one day. This means that in sociotechnical terms a 'whole task' should have a time dimension of at least one day. Nevertheless, many operations in primary processes seem to require much less than a day. But remember the story of the four stonemasons. The time perspective upon work done cannot be inferred from the actual time that people spend on the operation, but is related to their work capacity. If we take throughput time as a measurement unit for work , i.e. the time needed for fulfilling the requirements of a client, we are again able to relate time to work content. This is a radical departure from the way 'economic' theory measures labour: in hours, without referring to any result. For this reason, labour is seen as a pure cost instead of the basis of any added value.

Once the meaning of the work related to its added value has disappeared, the hour has been chosen as a relevant unit for the control of labour. Indeed, if the shortest time span is a working day, then organically the control frequency will be one tenth of it, more or less a working hour. The concept of productivity as output per unit labour has then become the surrogate aggregated measurement of added value. But the productivity measurement omits every reference to the meaning attributed by the beneficiary of the output of the work process.

About 30% of therapeutic activities in hospitals are treatments for iatrogenic problems, i.e. problems generated by the medical activities themselves. If health-system productivity is measured by the number of beds filled or by the number of patients treated per time unit we have a strong incentive to create sickness. Moreover, one of the major reasons why iatrogenic diseases become so important is due to the division into very short time slices of a healing process, which is perceived completely differently by the patient. The patient has become unable to 'manage' the 'whole task' of his or her treatment. The number of short (thus 'productive') diagnostic, nursing and treatment operations generated by the health system has become completely unrelated to the throughput time of the service required by the patient: the healing and nursing processes.

4.1.2 Volume Requirements

The volume is the number of items of a product or a service that are seen as a relevant unit for the customer. The requirements for producing 1000 items of a certain product are quite different from the multiplication by 1000 of the requirements to produce one item. The mathematical equation $1000 \times 1 = 1 \times 1000$ is invalid for systemic work systems. Batches have different systemic emerging characteristics as a function of their size. The added value of most distribution systems, from banking to retailing, consists of making products and services available in quantities which are required by customers.

The major change in the car-production industry during the past 10 years has been the achievement of the one-item batch. Instead of assembling a batch of 100 cars of the same model, a more or less fixed sequence of different models is assembled. The change in logistic requirements to permit this has had an impact upon the design of the car as well as upon the whole network of supplies and suppliers to the assembly line. The set-up time of an assembly line now has a different meaning.

Although the same chemical process can produce a liquid which can be bought by the tanker and in phials of a few centilitres, packing and distributing them through the same work system will lead to waste and quality problems. In the same way, the production of a broad range of products in a job shop is quite different from that of large batches of the same product in a production line. When both are combined in one work system, problems result.

However, providing credit to an individual or to a governmental agency is quite a different transaction, although the basic process is exactly the same.

An awareness of the importance of volume requirement has led to a review of the concept of economy of scale for manufacturing. This concept is based on a very restricted view of efficiency: the cost per unit produced can be reduced by investing in manufacturing installations able to produce more units per time unit. The costs of storing, distributing and, in general, of shaping the production as a function of the customer requirements have been omitted. The extremes to which this way of thinking lead are most apparent in the former Eastern bloc, where in fact ideologically added value did not exist. Production was undertaken without any direct reference to customers. In Lodz (Poland) there was a factory producing nylon stockings for the whole Communist bloc. However, even in Western economies short-sighted discounted cash investment calculations still lead to underused inflexible production facilities. In the literature on manufacturing strategies we meet increasingly the replacement of the concept of economy of scale by the concept of economy of scope.[1] Here the volume requirements of customers are a primary factor in the determination of the size of the production volume.

4.1.3 Quality Requirements

It is possible to produce a Rolls-Royce and a VW Beetle with the same technology. Nevertheless, the expectations of customers for both cars are completely different. A work system which tries to fulfil both kinds of requirements at the same time is doomed to fail: either the VW Beetle will become much too expensive or the Rolls-Royce will lose its intrinsic quality.

On the other hand, a Rolls-Royce customer will be prepared to wait for the delivery of a customized car, while a VW customer wants to drive home with a new car directly from the dealer.

A canned-food producer encountered problems when he started to fill his production capacity with both his own brand and the own-label product of a distribution chain. His customers became aware after a learning period that the only differences between the two products were the label and the price.

The intrinsic quality of a product or service is the emergent systemic quality, in which the customer places his or her appreciation of the product or service. Too often, products are perceived only from the viewpoint of production technology and the client's requirements are forgotten. This leads to problem-ridden and unmanageable work systems. If people express themselves in the results of their work, then the intrinsic quality of the products and services which they provide plays a very important part in producing their sense of work. They are aware of the added value, which they produce in the eyes of their customers. When these requirements are too widespread, they can no longer identify with their products, services and customers, and alienation begins.

Indeed, quality is at the core of the added value as perceived by the customers. The market can be considered as an ecological system, where there is a place for many different niches only because of the quality requirement. Economic theory is unable to understand these markets, when its models are based upon the linearity of preferences and the resultant utility curve. Intrinsic quality requirements cannot be divided into their components. Again, we are confronted with emergent systemic characteristics. The intrinsic quality of a product or a service is best treated systemically. The controversy between global and local markets can be approached by the concept of intrinsic quality requirements.

The problems of EuroDisney near Paris and the success of Disneyworld in Florida can be understood in the light of the fulfilment of intrinsic quality requirements, which are alien to a large number of the European customers targeted.[2]

Global products such as Coca-Cola and Heineken beer are produced with a local taste. One of their intrinsic qualities is their universal availability. But this is combined with 'local' taste.

4.1.4 Price requirements

The appreciation that a client has for a certain product or service is directly related to the price he or she is prepared to pay for it. This price can be expressed by money, goods or services, which require effort. It is the reverse side of the transaction coin, for which the intrinsic quality is the obverse. Added value is an attribution of the client, not of the producer, except in monopolies and other institutions which use coercive power against their clients. As in the case of the volume requirement, the mathematically equivalent formulas Selling price = Costs + Margin and Margin = Selling price − Costs are quite different in economic terms. The first formula is often used in production-oriented organizations, while the second is much more related to market-oriented ones.

Many Japanese manufacturing companies define selling price as the independent variable for the introduction of a product into the market. The challenge for producers is to make a product with a profit. In contrast, in former Communist countries the first formula is still much in use and the introduction of the free market does not lead to more efficiency by reducing costs but rather to a large increase in the selling price and a greater exploitation of customers as a result of distribution monopolies.

In open markets the cost is the variable to be managed in the work system itself. Here also the range of price requirements cannot be too large because the people in the work system cease to appreciate the relevant costs.

In the photographic industry two kinds of emulsion are used for processing. The expensive emulsion contains silver and the cheap one does not. In a given plant the workers and the supervisor viewed production management as their client and knew that their work was appreciated in terms of cost. One of the major production problems was the loss of material due to malfunctions of the equipment and these material losses were immediately translated into monetary terms. As the workers had no control over the nature of the product itself, they became confused. Their customers—production management—evaluated them adversely for what, for them, were minor losses of material containing silver while large losses of silverless material passed without notice. Once the losses were expressed in square metres of material they were able to satisfy their client.

The price that a customer is willing to pay for a product or service is not necessarily expressed only in monetary terms. How far a customer will travel, how long he or she is prepared to wait for the product/service can be important 'price' parameters. Once we start to look at added-value transactions in the non-profit sector, the definition of price requirements is completely different.

Because of the opacity of the tax system, the relation between governmental products/services and their users has lost any reference to its price. When customers receive the impression that services are provided free, dependency and counterdependency behaviour starts to colour the relation between supplier and customer. Quality and appreciation can no longer be valued. As a consequence, taxes will always be perceived as being too high in relation to the services provided, while those services will always be thought of as worse than they really are. This is one of the problems of public service.

On the other hand, one of the major services which organizations such as Greenpeace and Médecins sans Frontières are providing to their supporters is media coverage and they receive it free, as long as they are 'creating' news by their mere presence.

I am not pleading for a general privatization of public services. I separate the discussion of ownership from that of which kind of transaction a work system provides. If the transaction belongs to the added-value domain, then the price requirement of the customer has to be taken into account.

4.2 PROCESS LEVEL OR STRATUM 1: FROM 1 DAY TO 3 MONTHS

4.2.1 Generic Transformation Process

To materialize a specified output (product, service or a combination of both) with a prescribed means, technology and method in the most efficient way, i.e. with a minimum of waste. Efficiency is defined here (cf. Checkland[3]) as the realization of the process with a minimum of waste.

On this process level the desired output, the requirement of the client to be met, is sufficiently specified in terms of quality, delivery time and minimal cost. Also, the technology, the tools and methods to be used for achieving this requirement are prescribed. The only sources of variance in the process for which discretionary decisions have to be made are randomly occurring mismatches between reality and the given specifications of input, process and output. If input, process and output are overspecified, each variance will lead to a breakdown of the process and a delegation of the problem to the next higher process level, in which the specifications are made. If they are underspecified, the reliability of the process and its output are endangered. *It is clear that most activities on the shopfloor, referred to as primary processes, belong to this process level.*

Two comments are necessary to uncover activities that belong to this process level:

(1) When one walks through production plants, or looks at the transactions taking place in banks, clinics, shopping centres or transport systems, at first one is confronted with operations which are much shorter than a day. But the operations are only the visible elements of a process of a longer duration, certainly in the perception of the customer.

> Train commuters specify their need for getting to work and back home as one process. Many visitors to shopping centres have a shopping list for a whole week, they hate to have to come back for one reason or another. In the same way, many individual bank customers work on a monthly transaction with their bank. In production facilities, the unit of production is often not one item but the fulfilment of a daily and (much more often) a weekly production plan.

Thus the operations are in themselves not necessarily the place to consider for increasing efficiency or reducing waste. The whole process, with the right time perspective as perceived by the customer, has to be analysed in terms of efficiency. One of the most frequent causes of customer frustration is being confronted with the partial optimization of operations, constituting the whole process.

> The most tangible signs of suboptimized operations is the appearance of queues or stocks in a process. This applies as much to a motorway system, which can be defined as the shortest time between two queues, as to the sequence of queues, which are part of air-travel rituals. In factories, all material waiting for a subsequent stage is also a sign of inefficiency in the whole process. The tendency to structure production into flow lines is one of the ways to avoid suboptimization inefficiency.

(2) Some primary processes seem to last longer than 3 months.

> In Belgium the processing of a will takes an average of 5 months, from the certification of the deceased to the payment of taxes and the distribution of the estate to heirs. Even buying a house normally takes longer than 3 months if we define the process as starting from the decision to buy to moving in as an owner. If you have the house built it will take longer still.

Efficiency issues for these processes have to be divided into two process levels: the organization of the means necessary to perform the process and the efficient use of the means, once they have been chosen and organized. (See next process level.)

In the case of a will the means to be provided by the insurance companies of the deceased, the solicitor and the tax authorities must be streamlined before being put to work. If not, recalculations, repeated missing data, etc. will make the transaction inefficient.

In the case of building a house, architect, owner and builders will have to come to an agreement about the specifications before the building process can start to run efficiently.

4.2.2 Basic Strategic Dilemma

Can the required output be realized with a minimum of waste? The demand for efficiency for meeting a defined client requirement with the tools and methods at hand is satisfied in the processes taking place at this process level. Nowhere else can efficiency be achieved.

How many times does a worker in a primary process see that something is not working as planned but does not have the authority to take a decision to stop the process? Or how many times has he or she been told how to carry out an operation without any insight into the reason why, namely the customer requirements? The decisions which the worker takes when confronted with a process variance then lack the relevant context for action.

For this reason the output specifications related to the client's requirement must be made available as concretely as possible to the actors contributing to these processes. In the production sphere, models, dummies or photographs of clients using the products should be made available. There is no need to write long specifications or instruction manuals. Multisensory analogues are much more adequate. Learning the job with colleagues or showing videos are ways to form the carriers of the strategic information on this level. In the service sphere, a confrontation with real clients is very useful for sharing expectations and possibilities between clients and actors alike.

The staff of an organization's canteen arrange a meeting with employees who consume the meals. As a result of this meeting, the canteen workers become much more aware of the priorities of their customers so that they can cope with unpredictable variances which are always part of their daily work.

The producers of raw material or semi-products visit the works of their users. They have a joint meeting after the visit in which they clarify their mutual complaints and become much more aware of what is expected from the material they produce. An agreement is made between the supervisor on the supplier side and the supervisor on the customer side on how to deal with *ad hoc* and recurrent problems. Quality difficulties, which have been part of the discussions between managers of the supplier and of the customer for years, in this way are solved in 3 months.

The employees in a bank's office have a meeting with counter employees who deal directly with clients. Many office procedures, which have no longer any meaning for those doing them routinely are given a new context. Hence, some are discontinued, while others are performed much more efficiently, because the relation with customer requirements has been restored.

4.2.3 Control Information

There is a need to have a direct feedback about the present state of the required output and the waste produced in the process.

Many 'Japanese' production procedures such as kanbans, storage for goods and tools, clean workshops, discretionary powers of workers to stop a process when they see waste, etc. are carriers of control information on this process level. Process transparency is essential. When computers are used on this process level there must be a reliable linear relation between their output and the cause which created that output. Multiple possible interpretations of the control system's output and process itself may lead to disaster, as has been shown on Three Mile Island, in Harrisburg and, more recently, in the concerns of the Airbus 320 pilots. The availability of someone working on the next process level is essential: the integration of maintenance and production people in highly automated work systems is vital. The minimal frequency for monitoring the performance of these processes is once a week: weekly plans drawn as visual aids, weekly waste indications, etc. Waste has to be measured in units which are meaningfully related to its physical aspects: number of rejects, numbers of rework hours, number of customer complaints, length of queues and waiting time, square metres, kilos of material.

Monetary indicators are completely inadequate on this process level, because they require a double symbolic transformation before they can be understood: from the event to the physical parameter and then from the physical parameter to a monetary measure. Although this can be done very rapidly by data-processing equipment, the process to provide meaning to the monetary data needs a certain abstraction level for users. The current review of management accounting principles in the United States and in Europe takes this issue into account. The efficiency of Japanese manufacturing principles without the need for sophisticated cost accountancy has been the stimulus for this review.[4] Japanese companies have three times more workers per accountant than American ones. Conversely, they have twice the number of direct supervisors per worker. Apparently, they know intuitively that the only place where productivity and efficiency are really managed is on the shopfloor.

4.2.4 Audit Information

Reviewing the understanding of the output specifications and the standard procedures to achieve them and the analysis of waste patterns generated in the process.

Socio-technical variance analysis, i.e. an inventory of possible variances which can occur in the process and how they are dealt with by the people contributing to them, is an excellent tool for detecting sources of waste and for making the process more efficient (see Section 4.3). The introduction of quality circles is one of the common organizational forms by which these audit processes are fulfilled. The fact that the 'direct' workers are entitled to stop working and reflect upon what they have been doing and become observers of their own working principles implies that they are working on the next higher process level. This is typical of audit information processes. One of the underused tools in this context is audiovisual material.

A railway material maintenance shop was planning to build new facilities to increase its capacity. Searching for the right layout for the works, videotapes were made of the actual maintenance operations. These were used by the workers to review their maintenance activities. So many improvements resulted from this review that the need for new facilities disappeared. It is clear that the review could take place only after the workers were guaranteed their employment. The same number of workers could then cope with the increased workload. What they discovered was that this workload was not translated into more or harder work. On the contrary, after the analysis they were more at ease while they worked.

4.2.5 Development Activities

Debating the relevance of the several specifications to learn what are minimal critical specifications of the output, the input and the process itself, leading to more efficient work.

People contributing on this process level are the major clients of these specifications and should be entitled to debate their relevance for achieving the required performance. These debates should be held face to face, because understanding on this process level is not abstract. Behaviour is the most understandable information carrier.

There must be enough slack in the work system to permit these debates: time and space should be made available. Improvements are not to be stated in project terms: they are an ongoing activity belonging to the normal tasks of the actors on that process level. Continuous improvement belongs to the people working in it.

Because production is becoming increasingly capital intensive working in shifts is more common. If the workers are perceived only as hands, executing plans, and if the number of personnel has been calculated from this perspective, learning between shifts cannot take place. As no slack has been foreseen for these developmental activities, performance will suffer. This was one of the major findings in a diode plant, where certain diffusion processes took longer than one shift. The number of rejects was very large, because there was no way of measuring the performance of either shift against the customer requirements. In this way, the process was never under control.

4.3 PROCESS LEVEL 2: FROM 3 MONTHS TO 1 YEAR

4.3.1 Generic Transformation Process

To mould the specific requirements of the clients of the processes on process level 1 into minimal critical specifications regarding the output, the procedures, the tools and the input for those who perform the activities on level 1.

Already on this process level known clients have, in one way or another, to be involved to check the relevance of the specifications for their requirements. The fit between these requirements and their specification is the basic feedback loop on this process level. Here, for the first time, we encounter the difference between the users of the products of this level, i.e. the internal specifications and the requirements of the clients of the primary process, and the external clients, who specify what they want in terms of throughput time, volume, intrinsic quality and price. For this reason, the generic transformation process on this level is essentially a translation process.

I have experienced many times how product engineering departments producing mechanical parts require tolerances in their drawings which are not feasible using the technology available on the shopfloor. These fine tolerances are decided upon as a safeguard against what is perceived as the incompetence of the workers. They are not considered to be users of the specifications but as people who cannot be trusted, hence must be held under 'control' by strict instructions and specifications. After a while, the tolerances needed for the function of the part for the end-user and the specified tolerances by product engineering no longer bear any relation. Costs and frustrations soar. A vicious circle has been built in: the finer tolerances , the more they are unworkable.

One of the first indications that we are confronted with activities which belong to this process level is when questions arise on how resources have to be allocated and organized to reach certain targets.

Parenthesis 1: Short- and long-term allocation of capital

If allocation of resources belongs to this process level, with the time span of 3 months to 1 year, some light may be shed upon the debate which has been taking place in the United States since the late 1970s. Is the stock exchange and its obsession with short-term results an efficient way of regulating the allocation of capital to businesses? The answer that is given by the framework is definitely: yes. It is surprising that operational financial transactions do not belong to what we have called the added-value domain.

The basic misunderstanding in the debate stems from the belief that innovative activities are essential for the survival of sound businesses. As we will see later, such activities have a longer time span than those in the added-value domain. But if we refer to the example of the wine maker, Villa Antinori (see Section 3.3), and to many other successful small and medium-sized enterprises there is no need for a sound business to be involved in long-term costly innovative developments. A follower strategy is much more relevant for their success, as the Japanese economic revival in the 1970s and the 1980s has shown.

The concern at corporate levels about the need for capital-allocation efficiency and a long-term view, is no more than propaganda when contrasted with real behaviour. More people at corporate level are involved in short-term reallocation schemes, cost-cutting exercises and return on investment calculations than in long-term activities. Monthly, quarterly and annual reports are the most important and time-consuming ones for corporate and subsidiary employees. In many cases, longer-term 'plans' are no more than mere extrapolations of the actual status, coloured by either an optimistic or a pessimistic brush, according to the currently fashionable economic ideas. Corporate activities have much more to do with the power politics, which are linked to allocation issues, than with real efficiency and efficacy. Mintzberg,[5] Best,[6] Wheelwright and Hayes[7] and Piore and Sabel[8] are some of the authors who are demystifying corporate behaviour and its so-called allocation efficiency.

Parenthesis 2: Employment and other macro-economic schemes

My comments on the allocation of capital are also valid for macro-economic policies, which are expressed in terms of allocation or reallocation of resources. They are bound to be short term and belong to the second process level. In the 1970s Forrester of MIT[9], showed how, in spite of macro-economic policies, micro-decisions on the business level have a much greater impact upon the existence of all economic cycles, from the 5-year one to the Kondratieff cycle.

As a counter-example, we can refer to the Cybersyn experience of Beer[10] during the Allende years in Chile, where one of the strengths of the decision tools he designed was their avoidance of red tape and bureaucratic prevarications in making allocation and reallocation decisions at the level of the business sectors and individual businesses. In this way, the national economy was able to cope with the first transport strike in Chile without generating too many ripples after the transient event.

The fact that governments are increasingly making short-term reallocation decisions by changing tax schemes for businesses or the social security regulations every year is, in essence, sound behaviour. The only problem is that the way in which they do it does not take into account the systemic nature of the phenomena that they wish to influence. Indiscriminately, and by using only unsystemic aggregate data, they interfere on the wrong recursion level, in the added-value domain. In Chapter 6 we will give more details of governance and the value-systems domain.

These two parentheses are rather polemic in nature. But as the aim of the frame of reference I am developing is to shed new light upon the most diverse human activities, I hope that some readers will take up the challenge. If they are able to discover what the system really does, instead of accepting what it says it does, the frame becomes generative and may lead to innovative ways of dealing with the issues treated in the parentheses. As mentioned earlier, these innovations require a longer time span than the phenomena which belong to the added-value domain.

4.3.2 Basic Strategic Dilemma

Are the inputs to the process, the procedures and the tools still the best for meeting the client's specific requirements? The basic questions of efficacy (Checkland[3]) have to be asked here. Are we using the right means to achieve the result aimed at, the fulfilment of the client's requirements?

This means that on this level the allocation of time and money regarding the maintenance of the means of production and their improvement has to be balanced by the need for producing or servicing clients. Questions about redundancy in resources and people have to be answered on that level. The slack needed on the first process level for reaching the required specifications has to be discovered on this level. On this level also, for the first time, symbol manipulation is adequate. Quantified descriptions, specifications, targets, etc. start to be used in a relevant way. Performance indicators of all kinds can be used to express the strategic aims on that level[11]. Attributes of the client's requirements such as delivery or service time, intrinsic quality of the goods or services, quantities and cost are best used jointly, so that the tension or the apparent contradiction between them forces the actors in the system to look for ways of achieving a better balance between all of them.

In Total Quality Management programmes it is usual to measure performance by a composite index relating the delivery time, the quality and the cost of production. When the improvement in one parameter is at the expense of the other two, the composite index will show no improvement. All three aspects have to be improved at the same time (Figure 4.2).

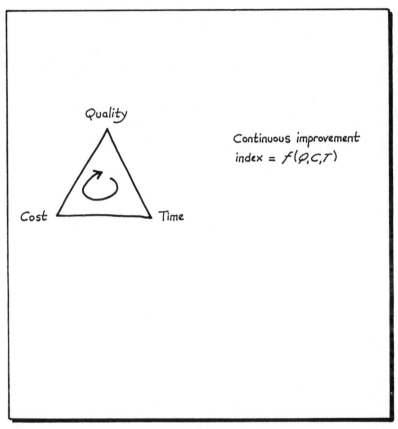

Figure 4.2 Components of a composite index for control and audit processes

4.3.3 Control Information

Two feedback loops must be monitored permanently. One relates to the transformation of the client's requirement in workable specifications. The other refers to the efficacy of the work system, the adequacy of the means used to achieve the output specifications.

This is the process level where follow-up indicators are best used to steer the resources when there are deviations in the desired results. The minimum frequency of monitoring this process is monthly, the maximum frequency is weekly. When reporting back is too frequent, oversteering may occur and the system on process level 1 may start to show a chaotic behaviour. When reporting is too infrequent, opportunities for discovering changing trends in the match between specifications and clients' perceptions of the results may be lost and may lead to the need for 'fire-fighting' when they do appear. Information technology can be used adequately to make reports by exception, filtering out such data which do not show a relevant deviation. Statistical process control in all its forms belongs to this level.

All kinds of graphic representation of time series, which show the target value of certain processes in relation to their actual value, are helpful to reallocate resources. Efficacy can be monitored through the time series of the mean time between failures, absenteeism levels, machine or installation usage, etc.

4.3.4 Audit Information

Here we can introduce the regular diagnostic procedures described in Section 2.2.3. The focus of the understanding of these processes must be on the fit between the resources made available to process level 1 and an understanding of the client's requirements.

Most formal audits—financial, quality, environmental, security, health, etc.— are performed once a year, which show that they belong to process level 2. Unfortunately, they are often perceived as inspection systems. The understanding then becomes how to avoid getting caught when the inspectors arrive—a very wasteful way of learning the wrong thing. The job of auditors and people alike working on that process level will become much more satisfactory when their contribution is seen as leading to efficacy improvements. One interesting form of auditing I have used is to organize visits by the people working on process level 2 in one process to colleagues in another process. Questions lead very easily to interesting discoveries.

There are interesting analogies between the logistics of all kind of 'refining' processes. These are processes which start from a raw material that shows a great variance in characteristics but which leads to a broad range of specific 'refined' products: the sorting out of second-hand clothing, the processing of corn into starch and glucose or of minerals into a broad range of pure metals and rare earths. People from these quite different branches of industry started to think in a different way about the 'waste', which seemed unavoidable. 'Waste' was turned into the term 'byproduct'.

4.3.5 Development Activities

All projects which lead to an improvement of specifications and the resources available on process level 1 belong here.

There is an interesting consequence to this statement. One finds regularly in the technostructure (i.e. those staff departments which have the task to improve the way processes on the first process level are done) people who introduce improvement projects which have a much longer planning horizon. Certainly, Information Technology projects, which were introduced merely as improvements on existing ways of working but which have continued for years, are an example.

When computers were introduced into production planning, purchasing and stock-keeping activities, in many cases the project was presented as the conversion of manual procedures into computer programs. In fact, the whole logistics were changed surreptitiously. Most projects lasted much longer than anticipated and the dissatisfaction of the users was not so much related to the poor quality of the project as to a feeling that the nature of the business was changing, without their being able to understand why and in which direction.

In fact, although they are presented as projects for this level, their consequences belong to other process levels and should be dealt with there. Time span and process level are ideal classification schemes to position projects, whatever their stated results.

4.4 PROCESS LEVEL 3: FROM 1 TO 2 YEARS

Here, we meet the highest level of the added-value domain and the lowest of the innovation domain, the next recursion level up (Chapter 5). Work systems are viable once they deploy activities related to the first three process levels. They can thrive and develop on their own, as long as they take care of the changing requirements of their clients, suppliers and employees.

Many former blacksmiths became motor mechanics, many tourist hotels were converted into seminar halls, many shops are only following the changes in fashion. The oldest known companies in Europe, which are mostly family-owned, belong to this class: wine makers, small-arms manufacturers, clinics, etc.

If it were not for the pathological obsession with growth in our economics ideology, rather than for a sound interest in development, organically most work systems, encompassing the added-value domain, would work as autonomous entities. Supplies of money, goods, machines and tools, and people could be dealt with on this level through a network of contracts, without any interference from 'headquarters', boards, shareholders and other 'governors'. In practice, sound business units are quasi-autonomous, in spite of all kinds of control rituals imposed by 'higher' levels.

The added-value domain encompasses the realm of economic activities. When one looks from the perspective of work systems, one only sees small and medium-sized businesses in the profit and non-profit sectors, which have as basic aims to maintain mutually satisfactory relations with major stakeholders, customers, suppliers and employees. These relations express themselves in products, services and money. These are the byproducts of the activities, which conserve and adapt the relational structure between the stakeholders.

This statement contradicts all functionalist discourse about organizations. It is for me, as a practitioner, a key for understanding what moves people to combine their efforts in sometimes apparently futile activities. The maintenance and adaptation of relations is at the core of economic activity, not the production of goods and services, or the creation and fulfilments of reified needs. The functionalist language is useful in normal cases, but one should not get trapped in it when major changes are occurring in the value-systems domain. False contradictions such as ecology versus economy, private enterprise versus public, free market versus planned economy cannot be transcended if the autopoietic nature of work systems is replaced by any kind of functional discourse, which defines the reason of existence of joint efforts only from outside the system.

Autopoietic organization of living systems is characterized in that they are continually self-producing.[12] If work systems are defined by means of an autopoietic organization, we say that all structural changes which they undergo and which do not destroy them have as a result the conservation of their organization, i.e. the conservation of the relations which determine their autopoiesis. Structural changes signify changes in the nature of the components of the work system, i.e. activities and interpersonal relations. The autopoietic organization is the same as long as the system is living. We will return several times to the autopoietic perspective on work systems. Once I began to integrate the autopoietic nature of work systems, the reference to organizational goals as an intervention into them gave me a completely different perspective. External goals and their changes became as a language part of the means of adaptation and conservation of the autopoietic organization.

When I use the approach which I develop in this section, I am always surprised at how people express the meaning of their combined work in two complementary dimensions. On the one hand, they like the idea of working for others, their clients, very much. They never have any difficulty in defining who their clients are. On the other hand, they include themselves in their list of customers. Their mutual relations are always part of the picture. But the most important discovery I have made, and have started to use consistently, is that the nature of the work towards their external clients is an expression of how they like to experience their mutual relations. In this sense, all meaningful work is art, i.e. an expression, a materialization of the desired relation of the artists with their environment.

4.4.1 Generic Transformation Process

Developing alternative products and services and alternative ways of meeting the requirements and needs of known clients. Taking care of the right balance between ends and means.

Here, for the first time, the requirements of the clients of the work system are not taken for granted but are related to underlying wants. There are activities deployed for improving and developing the existing products and services. For the first time, effectivity can be questioned: why are we doing what we are doing?

Which kind of clients may be interested to have both food and non-food articles in our distribution centre? Which clients prefer highly specialized workshops or shops, which prefer to find a range of generic products and services? Which patients prefer a specialist hospital or a general one, and why?

When we can answer these questions we can translate them into requirements for process level 2. Most literature on business or corporate strategy is in fact useful for answering these questions. Once the authors leave the added-value domain and try to define in the same terms strategies which belong to the innovation or even the value-systems domain they begin to be irrelevant.

The fashionable concept of 'third-generation research', promoted, for example by Arthur D. Little,[13] refers only to adaptation activities on process level 3. It has nothing to do with activities belonging to the innovation domain. The concepts around corporate strategy of Michael Porter[14] are relevant for small and medium-sized businesses. Once he applies them to 'corporations' or even to 'states', they become impracticable and thus unreliable.

4.4.2 Basic Strategic Dilemma

Choices have to be made to allocate means for alternative products and services for known clients and ways of meeting the needs of those chosen clients. How far and how late do we react to developments in our environment?

The Swiss watch-making industry received a severe setback when it decided that electronic watches were not watches at all but merely Japanese gadgets.

Before I know for certain what will be the fashion next season, I have to look for possible supplies of fabrics and textiles. I have to make my contracts at the right moment. The same kind of choice resides in all products and services prone to fashion: it is an organic phenomenon that fashion industries work on a development horizon from 1 to 2 years. All follower strategies have to be seen in this light: well-tried products and services, developed elsewhere, can be introduced for the clients of the work systems belonging to the added-value domain. In the same way, well-tested technologies and methods can be used as an alternative. These strategies belong typically to process level 3.

The actions to make the relevant strategic choices apparent on this level are: planning and contingency planning, simulations and 'what if' studies, marketing research, consumer preference inquiries, etc. The design of measuring tools and procedures for use by process levels 1 and 2 belong to this level. They translate the strategic choices into manageable measuring devices.

The management teams of the business units of Shell are employing a user-friendly version of the Industrial Dynamics simulation algorithm to quantify possible scenarios related to the future of their business.[15] The counter-intuitive outcome of these simulations is the material, which feeds the strategic debates between the managers.

As information technology becomes more a questioning and simulation tool than a mainstream data follow-up, then we are in the area of personal computers and strongly interactive multimedia aids. Research since the end of the 1980s on group interactions with computer-generated hypermedia has a future as a support for the management of processes on this level. The Operations Room, designed by Beer and Espejo[10] during the Allende years in Chile, has been a precursor to these tools. Fernando Flores and Terry Winograd[16] are working along the same lines.

4.4.3 Control Information

A systematic follow-up to see if our procedures, tools, machines, processes, inputs and outputs are starting to show 'strange behaviour'.

By 'strange behaviour' we mean persistent trends or discontinuities in relevant parameters. They indicate that some enduring change has taken place in the environment and that adaptive measures need to be taken. These are the steering actions which belong to this level. The monitoring frequency of the operations is, at most, once a month and at least once a quarter—again, a very organic reporting frequency. Monthly and quarterly reports are current in all kinds of business.

Short-term statistical forecast methods are adequate as tools for providing control information for this level. These provide short-term forecasts which filter out transient behaviour but anticipate statistically if there is a trend or a step in the behaviour of certain parameters. They do not explain why this happens but give a warning that adaptive action has to be taken. The best way to represent this information is as graphic time series with a short-term extrapolation for the following periods (Figure 4.3).

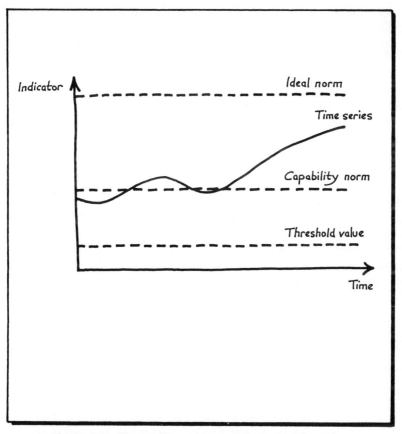

Figure 4.3   Time series and norms of a composite index

4.4.4 Audit Information

For the first time, purely internal audits are no longer sufficient. There is a need for regular (once a year or every two years) attendance at trade fairs, conferences, etc. to understand whether the activities deployed within the added-value domain still match what is happening outside it.

Organizational literature is a good barometer for seeing how the tension between *conservation*, e.g. maintaining our core business or core competences, and *adaptation*, e.g. flexibility, accelerated product design, customer-orientedness, etc. leads to impossible choices. As long as internal and external environments are seen as two separate realities[17] these will remain. To use the metaphor of Maturana and Varela in their Tree of Knowledge,[12] organizational theorists have great difficulty in avoiding the Scylla of representationism and the Charybdis of solipsism. Sometimes theorists write as if the organization is completely determined by its environment and preach a continuous adaptation to the 'changing' environment, as if the organization does not have any degree of freedom. Other theorists presuppose that if the internal coherence is kept, as long as the core competences of the organization are safeguarded, or as the 'human resources' are fully committed to the organizational aims and are exponents of 'the organizational culture', success and viability are guaranteed.

In terms of the VSM of Beer,[10] the audit information on this process level is strongly determined by the dialectical relation between what Beer calls the operational function (System 3 of the VSM) and the development function (System 4 of the VSM). In fact this dialectical relation generates the organizational closure (System 5 of the VSM) of the work system. In practice, an organizational audit on this level looks for the place of debate between both functions inside the work system. Because this process level contains the activities which belong to both the added-value and the innovation domains, these debates are characteristic of the identity function (System 5) of the work system.

In my practice as an organizational consultant I study what are called 'development' projects in a work system. I see how far these projects are left to staff specialists or external consultants, while the focus of the majority of the managers in the work system is to keep the business running as smoothly as possible. This indicates a work system in which the maintenance of what is the operational function is preponderant. My efforts are then geared to the creation of meeting-places where 'new' voices can be heard, without needing to start up new 'development' projects. Where many line managers spend much of their time in development work, I try to point to the history of the work system, so that priorities become more apparent and the operational aspects of the viability of the system return to the foreground. In work systems in the added-value domain this avoids the gap between management and workers, where management is perceived by the workers as operating in ivory towers, and management blames their employees for being resistant to change.

4.4.5 Development Activities

> *On this level we improve and adapt our products and services systematically and, if relevant, change our ways of providing them in terms of well-tested technologies and methods.*

Our activities and products and services have to remain 'fashionable' and be perceived as such by the stakeholders of the work system in the added-value domain. Improving products and services should be part of what is called 'continuous improvement'. In small and medium-sized businesses, where everyone has the opportunity to be in touch with customers and suppliers, this is self-evident. Only when contact with the environment becomes the functional prerogative of marketing and sales departments and the product development becomes the right of product engineering, or when other functional distinctions are made between inside and outside activities, is there a need for consciously creating development activities. These are then best done under the organizational form of projects, where in fact the various parties are enabled to meet each other across functional boundaries.

In corporations in the 'centralization' mood the development of improved products and services is 'delegated' to specialized research and development divisions. However, once work systems, business units with the right span of relations, are deprived of their development activities their viability is endangered. The place where the permanent adaptation of goods and services is occurring in sound organizations is where transactions with customers and suppliers are being made. Even when corporate structures are formally taking over these development activities, sound business units will continue to perform them in a hidden way.

A transport subsidiary of a large multinational asked me to sort out some of their organizational problems. As always in these circumstances (see Section 4.5.1), I tried to help them to define the nature of their business. During the exercise they found that by adapting continuously to new directives from headquarters in their relations with their customers, they had changed the nature of their business surreptitiously. Instead of providing transport, which now was left to a network of independent transport contractors, they had drifted into the business of organizing transport, and their major customers, apart from the parent company itself, were now other multinationals which had sold off their own transport subsidiaries. This was really a discovery for them. They were not aware that they had continuously adapted their services and developed new ones.

After this discovery, the small company (40 employees) started two actions. One was a marketing effort towards this kind of customer by renaming its activities 'logistic services' and by using new adequate advertising media. The other was a self-evident reorganization into major accounts, instead of the regional subdivision, which they had still retained from the original transport business.

4.5 APPLICATIONS AND INTERVENTIONS IN THE ADDED-VALUE DOMAIN

4.5.1 Defining Product Lines from the Viewpoint of Customers

In many firms working in the added-value domain I have found it difficult to define product or service lines. Those are mainly defined from the viewpoint of the unit producing them and not from that of the customer. This is certainly the case when the producing unit is separated from its customers. Marketing and sales units can be located elsewhere. Complex, opaque and hence generally superfluous distribution systems as trading agencies impede contact with customers. Where products are used in other products they are no longer recognizable by end-users, which is true for many industrial goods at the beginning of a long production chain.

To help these work systems to operationalize their strategies in the added-value domain it is essential that they are able to choose for which customers they generate added value. In fact, I have seen many times how the sales departments misunderstand customer-orientedness as the minimizing of their problems by passing a plethora of contradictory requirements to the production units and then complaining that production is not customer-oriented. No-one in the added-value domain can signify everything to everyone. Mutual satisfactory added-value relations are only possible between certain classes of suppliers and customers.

I use the attributes of work systems of the added-value domain, throughput time, intrinsic quality requirements, volume requirements and price requirements from the viewpoint of the *client, that is, the one who pays for the products or services,* and of the *end-user, that is, the one who consumes or works with them.* I ask a mixed team of salespeople and production engineers to make a table of the product/service/client/end-user combinations which show homogeneous characteristics in relation to these requirements. In many cases, even the sales people have to do some fact-finding to be able to use these concepts. Supplier and customer alike have learned to live with each other, even when both are silently complaining about the results of their relation: a mismatch between expectations and requirements has become accepted. Only when a competitor appears does the breakdown of the relation come as a surprise.

The Table 4.1 is also the basis for differentiating heterogeneous production units into semi-autonomous business units. Each small business unit is defined to fulfil the requirements of only one of the product lines, defined in this way. Internal customers and end-users can be defined in the same way. The network of customer–supplier relations becomes visualized and contracts can be reshaped between them. As a spin-off from this review many 'as if' co-ordination activities and problems disappear and an excellent basis has been created for implementing an Activity Based Costing[4] system, as a control system at process levels 2 and 3.

Table 4.1   Product-line form

	Throughput time	Volume	Quality	Price
Client 1				
Product/service 1				
Product/service 2				
...				
Client 2				
Product/service 1				
Product/service 2				
...				

In more general terms this method can help in discovering on which process level people invest effort. There is a tendency in organizations with geographically distributed services to create hierarchical levels, related to geographical zones. For example, shops or agencies are combined in a region. Different regions are combined into a district and different districts into an area. Each hierarchical level then becomes responsible for the sum of the underlying subdivisions. It is clear that the sum of work systems has no identity of its own and hence does not create added-value for anyone. Nevertheless, human beings try to create meaning out of their work, even if structurally they are placed in an impossible position. Under those circumstances, I use the method I have described with the managers involved. I ask the unit managers to define their major customers (maximum nine), and after that to define the services (maximum nine per customer) and their attributes, which they provide for these customers. Based upon the results of this joint inquiry, it becomes possible to define the 'business' they are in.

For a company distributing services, the area managers (an area consisted of a number of agencies) put their efforts into finding and coaching potential agency managers. In terms of the concepts they were developing activities on the second process level: defining, maintaining and creating the means (here, human resources) which are essential for the primary process. The agency was in direct contact with customers and suppliers and thus in charge of the primary process. Although formally the area managers were accountable for the profit and loss of the sum of the agencies, in practice, they invested no effort into this impossible task. The discovery of their added value was liberating for the group area managers. Without changing the formal structure, it became possible to function in a relevant way.

4.5.2 Process Analysis for Improving the Efficiency of Operations

As pointed out earlier, efficiency as the reduction of waste is the domain of process level 1, while efficacy or adapting the means and procedures to streamline the operations on level 1 belongs to process level 2. Once the parties involved in defining the products and services which are the reason for the existence of a work system in the added-value domain have been strategically defined, the following method can be used to translate this choice for the actors on process levels 2 and 1:

(1) A limited number of primary processes, significant for the strategy of the work system, are chosen for analysis. Remember that a primary process has been defined as consisting of those interdependent activities, which transform a demand of a defined customer (a product line customer of the previous method) into a fulfilment of this demand. All persons, independent of their actual organizational position who are contributing directly to such a process are brought together in one (large) room.
(2) The first task for the persons assembled in the room is to sit around a U-shaped table in the order they think their contributions are necessary for achieving satisfaction of the customer's demand. In bureaucratic organizations this generates much discussion, because interdependencies and their problems are mostly delegated upwards. In one firm there were 40 staff necessary for the processing of the customer's order onwards until its delivery and payment. The discussion lasted for three quarters of an hour but resolved many misunderstandings between the people involved.
(3) Someone takes the part of a customer and starts to ask questions to the people around the table. Where is my order now? How long and why have I to wait here? What is the added value for me of the operation you are performing? Why have I to pay for it? What can go wrong with my order here? Who in the chain is detecting the error? Who in the chain is correcting the error? etc.

Two things are happening during this exercise. First, because the person who plays the part of the customer is directly asking questions of everyone involved in satisfying his or her demand, the customer becomes a living being and not an abstraction. Embarassment and hilarity are present the whole time. The play aspect of the exercise allows laughter at these operations, which once had reason to exist, but have now lost their meaning. The tendency in organizations is always to add steps into procedures, never to prune them. Second, a rich amount of data becomes available for the people involved in process level 2 activities, which can help them to improve the procedures and methods for achieving customer satisfaction.

REFERENCES

1. Jellinek, M. and Goldhar, J.D. (1983). Plan for economies of scope, *Harvard Business Review*, **6**
2. Thompson, I. (1991). *The American Replacement of Nature*, Doubleday Currency
3. Checkland, P. and Scholes, J. (1990). *Soft Systems Methodology in Action*, Wiley
4. Kaplan, R. (1990). *Measures for Manufacturing Excellence*, Harvard Business Review Press
5. Mintzberg, H. (1983). *Power in and around Organizations*, Prentice Hall
6. Best, M. (1990). *The New Competition*, Polity Press.
7. Hayes, R. and Wheelwright, St.(1984). *Restoring our Competitive Edge*, Wiley
8. Piore, J.M. and Sabel, Ch. F. (1984). *The Second Industrial Divide*, Basic Books
9. Forrester, J. (1980) Inflation and unemployment, Invited Lecture 6th International Conference on System Dynamics
10. Beer, S. (1981). *The Brain of the Firm*, 2nd edn, Wiley
11. Hoebeke, L. (1990). Measuring in organizations, *Journal of Applied Systems Analysis*, **17**, University of Lancaster
12. Maturana, U. and Varela, F. (1987). *The Tree of Knowledge*, Shambhala Publications Inc.
13. Roussel, A., Saad, K. and Erickson,T. (1991). *Third Generation R&D*, Arthur D. Little, Inc., Harvard Business School Press
14. Porter, M. (1990). *The Competitive Advantage of Nations*, Free Press
15. de Geus, A. (1988). Planning as learning, *Harvard Business Review*, March/April
16. Flores, F. and Winograd, T. (1986). *Understanding Computers and Cognition*, Ablex Publishing Corp.
17. Quinn, R.E. and Rohrbaugh, J. (1983). A spatial model of effectiveness criteria: towards a competing values approach to organizational analysis, *Management Science*, **29**, No. 3

Chapter 5

_ The Second Recursion Level: the Innovation Domain

5.1 BASIC DESCRIPTION OF THE INNOVATION DOMAIN

Process level 3 (1 to 2 years) is a hinge level. It is the major recipient of the products and services discovered in level 4 (2 to 5 years) and level 5 (5 to 10 years). From level 4 onwards there is a change in the nature of the activities. The activities on levels 3, 4 and 5 form their own organizational closure, they have their own emergent output and process characteristics. Work systems in the innovation domain have their own way of maintaining and adapting their essential relations, their autopoiesis. For this reason, we can speak of a new recursion level in terms of Beer. The primary characteristic of the actors working in that domain is that they are involved in *the process of consciously creating the future*. As Ackoff[1] writes, they are behaving in a proactive mode. The time span of the innovation domain stretches *from 1 year* when we take into account the overlapping role of level 3 *to 10 years*. I use the term 'innovation' because of the creative process which defines the domain. The basic process which belongs to this domain can be described as follows.

Changes in values in the environment in which the work system in the innovation domain is embedded are sensed and transformed into new products, services and processes. The work system is involved in the discovery and the creation of the added-value of the future.

It is clear that the clients and end-users of these kinds of product and service are not yet known. For this reason, the concept of client has to be broadened into one of stakeholder. By defining the stakeholders, we determine the quality of the infrastructure which will permit the realization of the working and living networks of the work systems in the added-value domain of the future. The stakeholders of work systems in the innovation domain will suffer or benefit from the creations which are expressions of accepted or unaccepted changes in values (Figure 5.1).

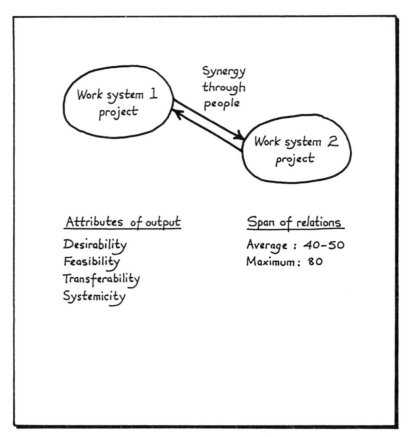

Figure 5.1 The innovation domain

The innovations to which I refer are not limited to the fulfilment of existing needs, they are expressions of new desires. In business jargon, one could say that the improvements of products and services which are developed on level 3 are pulled by the 'market', while the work systems in the innovation domain are pushing, creating new 'markets'. In the previous 200 years most work systems in the innovation domain were embedded in a technological environment, because the underlying value in society was modernism, which saw the expression of science in technological innovations as the hallmark of progress. At the end of this century, this world view is increasingly being criticized. In Chapter 8 I will go into more detail about system innovations, which are related to 'post-modern' or 'post-industrial' values.

The relation between innovations and value systems is best exemplified by Marshall McLuhan in his *The Gutenberg Galaxy*.[2] The co-evolution of linear causal world views and the dissemination of the written word through printing technology is one example. The co-evolution of 'holistic' world views and the distribution of images through printing and then through electronic visual media is another.

The tensions in contemporary financial systems can be interpreted as the transition of methods of exchange, which were dependent upon material flows in space and time, towards exchanges which have become purely symbolic and can travel with the speed of light, introducing a quasi-simultaneity. Financial systems and virtual worlds co-evolved into a completely new way of giving things value. Both are expressions of the post-modern values.

Here also we can give some output criteria of the generic transformation process in this domain. The realization of these output criteria by the work systems of the innovation domain is a necessary but not sufficient condition for the success of an innovation. We call an innovation successful when it becomes integrated into the work systems of the added-value domain in the environment of the innovation. Because of the fact that the work systems in the innovation domain belong to a higher recursion level, they can only create necessary conditions. The autonomy of the work systems of the lower recursion level, the added-value domain, is the constraint which creates the sufficient conditions. Although there is a tendency in the literature on innovations to find the philosopher's stone to account for their success, the systemic nature of the relation between innovation and added-value domain implies the futility of this quest. A successful innovation can only be called *post hoc*.

For this reason, it is not surprising that people who feel at ease working in the innovation domain are not inclined to use the words 'success' and 'failure'. The inquiry process in itself is what they value most. High-performing Research & Development divisions are exempt from the fear of failure. When innovative efforts fail, they are perceived as necessary learning elements. Statistically, only 15% of innovative projects which are formally started come to fruition.

The anecdote about Thomas Edison, who was testing the two-thousandth alloy for the filament of his electric lamp is typical in this respect. When his laboratory assistant asked him to stop his research after so many failed attempts, he answered: 'At least, now we know how not to do it in 1999 ways.'

5.1.1 Desirability

The futures which will be discovered and invented must meet underlying changes of the value systems. The future must essentially have *an ethical and aesthetic attractiveness for the stakeholders* who will have to be involved in its further realization and use. This is only possible if *the innovators themselves have a passion to achieve what they desire. Desirability then becomes an attribute of a relation between innovators and stakeholders. It can be measured by the degree of positive effort that both make in that relation.* The desirability criterion may shed light upon the difficulties that economic theory has with innovations. The economic world view focuses mainly on needs. Products and services are seen to fulfil customer needs. There is no need for innovations, they are the expression of desire. People committed to them wish to express something new in a product or service. It is only when innovations become common that they can be included in the set of needs.

When Watson was confronted with the results of a classical marketing research for the use of computers in business environments, which showed an almost non-existent market, he put the results aside. He believed in the desirability of the new product and created the market. He used very cleverly the desire for control that managers on the highest levels of the new 'big' enterprises and multinationals valued. The IBM sales technique did not focus upon the users of the new technology but upon those managers who were not even interested in the new technology as such. Watson successfully sold quasi-control and quasi-certainty.

5.1.2 Feasibility

Innovation always has to pass through a Machiavellian struggle: those who have to defend the present know what they have to lose, while those in favour of the innovation are, at most, lukewarm champions. What they can appreciate is still pie in the sky. And they are very aware that there can never be given any guarantee that the new state of affairs will succeed. The dialectic tension between the 'conservatives' and the 'innovators' leads to a feasible (i.e. socially and culturally acceptable) expression of the innovation. *Here again, feasibility is an attribute of the relation between innovators and stakeholders. It can be measured by the degree of defensive effort that both invest in the relation.* In contrast to positivistic scientific ideology which claims that scientific endeavours are value-free, one finds in scientific innovative environments much rhetoric, apologetics and debate. This is a healthy state of affairs. It is a way by which work systems show a sound resistance to change. Not every brilliant or maverick idea can be assimilated.

In the project management literature the first stage of an innovation project is called a 'feasibility study'. When the outcome of the study is expected to give a guarantee of the success of the project, the study will continue indefinitely. More analysis will be needed and more resources will be put into preparatory explorations of opportunities and threats.

The public agencies involved in development work in Third World countries, and now in the former Communist bloc, are known for their production of red tape, which is not commensurate with the work that is actually done. It is as if a project is a stumbling block between a feasibility study and an evaluation study. It is clear that a bureaucratic culture, where legitimation and justification are more important than action, is not a very adequate environment for taking risks to start activities which intrinsically have no guarantee of success.

In the light of the definition of work systems in the innovation domain, the major task of a feasibility study should be to try to influence the major stakeholders of the project so that its results become politically and culturally acceptable. How do I, as champion of the innovation, transfer minimally my desire to achieve it to the various parties involved?

5.1.3 Transferability

The balance between desirability and feasibility is the substrate for creating the conditions in which innovations can be assimilated by the work systems in the added-value domain. *The degree to which an innovation can easily be spread in the added-value domain gives an indication of its transferability.* Many innovations fail because too few efforts are made to achieve transferability. The major psychological hurdle with which innovators are confronted is to relinquish their ownership. This is the fate of many 'entrepreneurial' innovators. Only if the innovation is left as an inheritance to the work systems in the added-value domain will it become successful.

It came as a great surprise to researchers in a high-tech lab that the purpose behind their endeavours had to be communicated clearly to their sponsors and potential users if they wanted continuous financial support. Their target for communication was almost exclusively the 'inner' circle of other research labs. They had created between them an esoteric language which safeguarded their ownership. Once they had to make the results of their work accessible to a broader group of stakeholders, they came under pressure to be ahead of them. Transferability is perceived as a threat to the power base of innovators. It also creates a demand that, once one is involved in innovations, one must continue to innovate.

In Africa, development agencies have tried for many years to introduce the use of tractors in agriculture. Therefore their major focus was on the training of men in rural communities. Blinded by their Western cultural background, they belatedly became aware that women are the base of an agricultural economy in Africa. The choice of the wrong stakeholder has been a hindrance for the transferability of the innovation.

It is interesting to analyse the concept of intellectual property as a way to inhibit transferability. Perhaps we are confronted here with a beautiful self-regulating mechanism, which limits the number of successful innovations in a 'progressive' business world, which gives much lip-service to innovations, but which rightly is anxious about too many of them. The abundance of regulations around innovations in the pharmaceutical industry can also be seen as 'healthy' defences against the innovation ideology which reigns in this business. Of the 7500 annual applications for new pharmaceutical products, less than 1% are really innovative. The time necessary for the introduction of a new product is actually about 15 years, which is an indication that regulation has become counterproductive. Remember that the innovation domain has a maximum time span of 10 years.

5.1.4 Systemicity

As innovations recreate a new conceptual order in their area, the classification schemes of the old order are no longer valid. Hence it is essential to take into consideration the innovation area within its context. *The degree in which an innovation has been conceived, taking into account the interfaces with other areas, is an indicator of its systemicity.*

The introduction of Information Technology into the financial world has completely changed the nature of financial business. Only 5% of the daily international money transactions relate to its basic added-value: covering exchanges of goods and services. 95% is purely speculative and highly symbolic. The turmoil created by this has never been thought through: self-regulating mechanisms are dealing with it, which means that, among other consequences, there is hardship for the majority of the people in the Third World. The basic intention of introducing this technology was to be able to do more in a shorter time. It was not perceived to be an innovation with the systemic consequence that the nature of the business changed profoundly.

When working on the 'car of the future', many companies do not take into account that a car is only one possible means of transport. They do not even think that the underlying value trend among professionals, one of their major 'markets', is to reduce mobility, to work at home, linked with colleagues by data and multimedia networks. The car makers only take into account actual concerns such as pollution and accidents. Most of the 'innovations' in the car-making industry still belong to the third level of the added-value domain.

The 'electric' car, which, at the same time, considers the development of accumulators and of a distribution network for recharging them, must be seen as an example of systemicity in its area.

When Steve Jobs started his adventure with Apple Computer he received the same reception in the existing computer industry as the Japanese electronic watch did in the world of the Swiss watchmakers. 'This is not a computer', as 'This is not a watch'. He struggled to get his concept accepted and created a whole new computer business, which at last had to be accepted by IBM. He changed not only the nature of the computer business but also the basic valuing of information technology in society.

For this reason marketing research is quite different in the added-value domain from the innovation one. The first focuses upon existing customers, the second upon trends in values in society: customers cannot yet be defined.

5.2 PROCESS LEVEL 3: FROM 1 TO 2 YEARS

In the added-value domain, we have stated the basic strategic dilemma for this level as follows.

Basic strategic dilemma: choices have to be made to allocate resources for alternative products and services for known clients and alternative ways of meeting the needs of those chosen clients. How far and how late do we react to developments in the environment?

When put into the innovation domain this dilemma can be described in a complementary way.

Choices have to be made for alternative products and services in which known clients could be interested. Do we take the risk of reformulating the needs of those clients through these novel products or services?

Thus in process level 3, because it is the link between the added-value and the innovation domains, we are confronted with the basic dilemma between innovation and adaptation for existing clients and 'markets'. The way in which this dilemma is normally expressed is by what is known as 'pilot projects'. The result of these trials is in fact the first check whether the proactive anticipation of the needs and wants of these clients are minimally met by the novel products and services, developed on a small scale. This is a well-known method for technological innovations. The question can be asked why the same way of working is used so seldom for organizational, social and political innovations. When the word 'reform' is used in this context, it refers mainly to grand schemes. This may be a way of coping with the intrinsic resistance of the 'Establishment' when confronted with an ideology in which innovation, change and transformation are seen as a 'must'. Attempting grand schemes is then the best way to change nothing by proving that social innovation is impossible on such a scale.

Since the late 1970s there has been a sequence of organizational trends such as 'the search for excellence', 'total quality management', customer-orientedness, organizational culture change, the learning organization, downsizing, business reengineering, etc. which were introduced through large training programmes in many corporations. The rhetoric about the necessary innovations thus created an auto-immune reaction among the people within these corporations. In many companies, only the rhetoric has changed, nothing else. The French have a saying: 'Plus cela change, plus c'est la même chose'—the more it changes, the more it stays the same.

Because of its crucial position, activities on the third process level are the litmus test for innovations. In terms of time span, 1 year is one tenth of the maximum time span of 10 years for innovative activities. As we defined earlier, this is the correct frequency for monitoring the innovation processes of level 5.

5.3 PROCESS LEVEL 4: FROM 2 TO 5 YEARS

5.3.1 Generic Transformation Process

Transforming the signals of change in the value systems of the major stakeholders into new generic products and services which, at the same time, make this change perceptible to them. They reveal concretely the future which is already present and shape it in that way.

The great canal, tunnel and railway builders in the second half of the nineteenth century were making possible the migration of workers from rural areas and the new urbanization. They expressed the loss of community life, embedded in the philosophy of the Enlightenment, which focused upon the preponderance of the individual. They made full use of the combined inventions of the previous decade: the manufacture of precision mechanical parts, new methods of steel making, the use of steam as an energy source.

A major part of Japanese industry after the Second World War was geared to create the Japanese counterpart of the American middle class: an example they took from their conquerors. The car, consumer electronics, photographic and electric domestic appliances industries, the success stories of post-war Japan, are directly related to the stereotypes of the American middle class.

The whole cinema industry started from the first decade of this century onwards to meet the dilemma posed by an official puritanical anxiety concerning intimacy and the public's desire for that intimacy in an anonymous urban context: a white screen and a dark theatre.

I give this last example to make clear that innovation has not to be seen only as a purely technological event: innovations may take place in every area. There is a technological component, but this is not necessarily the most important one.

The Live-Aid concerts need satellite television transmission but they are an innovation in their own right. In the same way, the daily newspaper can be seen as an innovation, although it uses a known technology: printing.

Innovations should not be confused with inventions. Successful innovations, after their first introduction to new clients, generate many followers in the added-value domain.

The invention of the Solvay chemical process to make sodium hydroxide and its derivatives became an innovation once Solvay started to build factories near alkali mines worldwide. They were one of the first 'multinationals'. Solvay innovated by guaranteeing the coherence of its image as a multinational by using the same system as the colonial empires. The intensive and lengthy training of their engineers and potential site managers created a coherent social class, analogous to religious orders or the administrators of the Raj. Solvay created a 'business' empire.

Therefore transferability in all its dimensions is needed. The focus upon the relations between added-value work systems and level 4 is essential. This can be expressed by the following basic strategic dilemma.

5.3.2 Basic Strategic Dilemma

Attachment to or detachment from what already exists is the dilemma confronted by innovators active on recursion level 4.

On level 3, product, service and process improvements are organically developing through a normal learning curve; the strategic choice on level 4 is to risk creating a discontinuity. In many cases this risk has been taken surreptitiously: real innovations have been introduced in the guise of improvements. I mentioned earlier the introduction of data communication and information technology into financial business. As another example the development of medical diagnostic technology has unobtrusively changed the task of the doctor and basic processes in hospitals. Somewhere a threshold has been passed unnoticed. Many problems in the domain of hospital care and its organization become apparent only with hindsight. From a nursing aspect, hospitals have become medical factories, processing patients or even parts of them. For that reason, most hospitals have become riddled with management and organization problems. The gap between what the work system says it does and what it does has become too large. Adapting the old ways of organizing hospitals is not enough. An organizational discontinuity is required. The question is not where decision power has to be placed, whether with the medical staff, the nursing staff or the administrators. It is: if the discontinuity in the primary process, from a nursing work system, where the patient was the most important actor to a patient-processing work system, where medical technology and its professionals have become the major actors, is desirable and feasible in relation to actual current views upon health and illness.

The major reason for these surprises is that many innovations do not score well on the fourth attribute I mentioned: systemicity. This is due to the confusing of development in a specialized field or discipline with innovation, which takes into account the work systems in the added-value domain which already exist or have to be created to assimilate the innovation.

It is only now that silicon wafer production outside the laboratory, in industrial environments, is giving appropriate yields. The care required for high-tech laboratories had to be conveyed to industrial workers. The processes are still non-transparent. In many cases there is insufficient monitoring of the qualities of the silicon wafers due to the technical difficulties of measuring them during processing. The laboratory operators had a feel for that quality. Workers were not initiated into it.

For this reason, two pathways have to be followed for getting the relevant strategic information onto level 4: scanning the ideas and concepts which are generated by levels 5 and 6 (see later), because they are the source of innovations as I define them here. On the other hand, because the distance between what can be and what is, is the major parameter to decide for innovation (detachment) or not (attachment), a good knowledge in the development of work systems in the added-value domain is essential.

The difficult relations between centralized research and development divisions and the business units, for which they are supposed to work, can be seen as the organizational expression of this strategic dilemma. If this tension is perceived as negative by management, and if, for that reason, the two levels of activities are separated from each other organizationally or even geographically, then transferability and systemicity come under threat.

One last comment: many so-called innovations do not belong to this level. I hope that the examples given help the reader to distinguish innovations from improvements. Innovations, even though they find a fertile soil to develop once they start, are nevertheless discontinuities. They have a totally different quality from what already exists as process, product or service.

Cinema and theatre are radically different from each other. Road building through a landscape is radically different from following a landscape. Newspapers are radically different from printing copies of manuscripts.

5.3.3 Control Information

The reaction of the stakeholders and the timely detection of new stakeholders have to be monitored.

The entrepreneurial risk of allocating large amounts of resources in new ways, products and services requires a timely influence upon the relevant stakeholders in a proactive way. Reacting is not enough. Monitoring steers the proactive actions: lobbying, advertising, using the media, etc. Control information should be monitored maximally every quarter, minimally every half year.

Although much of the project management literature emphasizes the use of quantitative data for the follow-up of innovative projects, in practice they are not so relevant. Resources such as time, money, person-months have to be seen as limits, as constraints much more than as follow-up indicators. When the project is going beyond the limits of its resources, questions about its continuation become relevant. As mentioned earlier, success can never been guaranteed. One of the major skills needed in the management of innovative projects is to be able to stop them in time. A few quantitative indicators which refer to the resources that are still available are helpful in determining the right moment for the go–no-go decision.

But these are extreme decisions. The ongoing monitoring of the four attributes of the innovative project—desirability, feasibility, transferability and systemicity—is quite different in nature. Innovations are best organized into projects and the project team members are the most adequate providers of these monitoring data. The reason lies in the uncertainty which always accompanies innovative activities. The antidote for dealing with uncertainty is sharing it with trustworthy colleagues. And trust is built up when the members of a group are able to deal with differences in views and contributions. The tension between desirability and feasibility is also embodied in different members of a good project team and is an opportunity for having strong but constructive conflicts. The debates in such a project team help the members to be sensitive to signals from their environment, and the ambiguity of the signals motivates them to influence the stakeholders in that environment through sharing and comparing the different interpretations of these signals. The relation between project team members and the various stakeholders in their environment is the adequate place for taking steering action.

An innovative organization placed the leaders of project teams involved in the development of new products formally into two groups. One consisted of various functional managers such as sales and marketing, service and production of the business unit, for which the innovation was meant. They were also members of 'research' teams, which were composed of technological gatekeepers. They were scanning the scientific community for relevant innovative technologies. In fact, the project leaders were thus structurally involved in process levels 3, 4 and 5. In the project group, which was focusing on activities on level 4, they introduced the signals of the other two relevant levels.

Uncertainty and ambiguity can only be dealt with in small and large groups. For this reason, project groups should never exceed 80 members. In practice, groups of 40 to 50 members are working best. They consist of small subgroups, which take care of the creative aspects of the work, but are embedded in a network of other subgroups, who have rather a braking function. Some may introduce standardization criteria, others patent or other regulatory aspects. When a project team consists only of enthusiastic champions of the innovation, the monitoring and the steering of the transferability and systemicity attributes will be neglected.

5.3.4 Audit Information

This is the first audit which has to ask whether the systems in the added-value domain are really doing what they say, and whether we understand the meaning behind any discrepancy, based upon our knowledge of changing value systems.

This is an essentially ethical question: how much of a lie is still acceptable, or how much incongruency and cognitive dissonance can we tolerate in the stakeholders of the operational domain? If these are too large, we find a strong incentive to defend a case on level 5. On this level outlines of alternatives should already be available.

There is a strong need to start to be inventive regarding the organization of the state and to do something about the felt discrepancy between living and working in a democratic society and the felt impotence when confronted with the media and governmental agencies. Where do we see successful experiments which are dealing with this issue? Stating repeatedly that Parliament should be reformed or that a public service should become more efficient no longer suffices. Here again institutional innovations are more important than technological innovations. But if the electronic media already play an essential role in the malaise concerning governance why should they not be included in whatever new community service institution we try out? (See Section 8.2.4.)

Inquiries of a general sociological kind and intelligently devised censuses using sophisticated statistical techniques are part of the adequate tools for this kind of audit. Expert panels of innovators are then confronted with these data and debate the meaning they attribute to them. The result of the audit information available in this level is an understanding whether the new products or services under development are in fact not introducing the need for a broader system innovation, an innovation which belongs to process level 5.

The introduction of Information Technology in the relation between industrial suppliers and customers is requiring a thorough change in the interorganizational relations between them. EDI (Electronic Data Interchange) is more than a procedural and technological innovation. It creates a discontinuity in the traditional way of dealing between customer and supplier.

5.3.5 Development Activities

Activities whose objective is to introduce and disseminate innovative products and services belong to this level.

Perhaps it is necessary to clear up some of the semantic ambiguities concerning the concepts of research, development and innovation, which are current in the management literature. I have used the generic term 'innovation' to point to a discontinuity in the order of things of a certain domain. Clearly, the creation of a new market through the introduction of a new service or product is an innovation. But in business terms, activities which lead to the introduction of new products or services are called development activities, in contrast to research activities, which result in discoveries or inventions. Following this terminology, the activities, which belong to process level 4 are development activities.

The sales of non-financial insurance, such as car or fire insurance, etc. in commercial bank agencies was an innovation and required about three years, on average, to be established. Insurance services already existed but were outside the domain of financial services. The banks' customers had to learn that insurance could also be considered as a service given by the banks. This learning process is part of the activities which take place on process level 4. In banking terms, insurances were called new products and the activities leading to their introduction were product development activities.

Parenthesis: Research

The term 'research' is much more ambiguous. Sometimes research activities are seen as those activities necessary to arrive at a go–no-go decision about the introduction of a new product or service. In these circumstances they belong to what we called a feasibility study. Most research activities in business belong to this class and hence to process level 4. Nevertheless, many research programmes have a longer time span than 5 years. The framework which I develop here may help an understanding of the basic differences between activities which are commonly called research.

Many research efforts which are done in specialist areas at universities or in private laboratories are in fact nothing else than what Kuhn[3] has called 'normal' science. They are aimed at the confirmation of existing models and theories and are essentially conservative in nature. In fact, innovation is the least of the concerns of these efforts. In contrast, the publishing of the results of this kind of research has to pass through a filtering process of reviewers, which have as a major criterion not disturbing the established 'body of knowledge'. Here again, we are confronted with a sound self-regulating mechanism, which, by using the language of scientific progress, rejects a possible overload of innovations. The growth of new disciplines and specialisms, the lip-service paid to the objectivity and the value-free stance of science, is the most certain path towards results, which score very low on the attributes of desirability, feasibility, transferability and systemicity. Elsewhere[4] I have argued that this kind of research should not be called fundamental but, rather, elementary. Its focus is the elements of the domain of specialization: physical particles, biochemical reactions, elementary stimulus-response behaviour, etc.

Only a small part of research activities is geared towards a new understanding of phenomena in the domain of research. Researchers involved are working on new models, theories, languages, world views. This kind of activity belongs much more to the value-systems domain. The prime concern is not to transform this new understanding into innovative products or services. As in art, the main objective is to express new ways of valuing the relations of people with nature or with each other. I will return to these activities in Chapter 6. It is this kind of research that may be correctly called fundamental.

Research activities which belong to process level 5 aim at 'inventions'. This means that the languages, models and theories developed by fundamental research are consciously used for creating innovations, which can lead to whole-system changes. In a business context we are confronted with innovative entrepreneurs and their teams. Thomas Edison is one of the best-known examples. But the same entrepreneurial spirit can express itself in a new constitution and corresponding political organizations. Benjamin Franklin, Thomas Jefferson and Napoleon Bonaparte are well-known examples of this kind of 'entrepreneurial' researcher. After this parenthesis, we are ready to develop process level 5.

5.4 PROCESS LEVEL 5: FROM 5 TO 10 YEARS

5.4.1 Generic Transformation Process

Sensing the changes in value systems, to recreate conceptually whole systems which reflect these changes and thus to create conditions for the introduction of innovative products and services relevant to these changes. On this level the rules of the game for the next decade are consciously made.

This is the highest level where decisions and choices are aimed at implementation in the added-value domain. It is also the level on which the paradigm shifts which are taking place in the next higher domain receive their form. It is the highest 'executive' level. Laws, regulations, working principles, technological infrastructures are decided upon for implementing a system change. The changes are system-wide and can no longer be encompassed by one domain of activities. Many organizations, governmental agencies, businesses, universities and research institutes contribute to the realization of a blueprint of the future.

A set of activities: lobbying, financial transactions, the creation of political and environmental awareness has made the Channel Tunnel possible. Already the relationship between the British Isles and the Continent is shifting. Real estate in the Pas-de-Calais and in south-east England is flourishing. Ferry companies are reorienting their strategies.

One can look at the practical infiltration of the environmental awareness during the last decade: many businesses and agencies have created a new infrastructure able to deal with the new ecological tenets. Some companies, which have only been reacting to the new regulations without sensing their spirit, have already missed the boat and are doomed to disappear in the coming decade.

Innovations which belong to this process level always imply many work systems. The focus of the innovative activities is upon the redesign of the relations between these work systems. One kind of interorganizational network is transformed into another. A technological invention may be the trigger for such an innovative effort, but designing new rules of the game between the components of the network and learning to work with them makes the introduction of the invention successful. And rules of the game cannot be altered if they are not in tune with the changing values of the various stakeholders in the network.

5.4.2 Basic Strategic Dilemma

Although immediate results are not available to verify choices, the efforts deployed on this level create a point of no return—in technical terms a bifurcation point.

These choices can cause many beneficiaries and many victims among the stakeholders, and one is not sure who will be what. The tension between the attractiveness of the future which is designed, the aesthetic aspect and the ethical aspect, the amount of unavoidable harm which will be caused requires most attention for those consciously involved in this kind of process. As the rules of the game are altering, the future pattern of winners and losers is also changing.

Sometimes this kind of systems transformation occurs as a random mutation.

After the oil crisis of 1973 in a period of less than 10 years house insulation had become a normal practice and had reshaped part of the building and glass industry. Public consciousness, media coverage and tax incentives, among other things, created the infrastructure for this change. A political price decision for crude oil created a bifurcation point, a point of no return in the building industry. The oil crisis matched perfectly the first generally widespread questioning of the 'throw-away' consumer society.

When I refer to a whole-system transformation it has to be distinguished from a worldwide transformation.

The series of conscious measures which has been taken by all the stakeholders in, for example, Zurich, to eliminate the car from the city centre is also a 'whole-system' change.

But transformation limited by formal organizational boundaries will rarely be seen as a 'whole-system' change. The organizations of the stakeholders have to change at the same time and more or less at the same pace. From there stems my reticence to follow the fashion of transformational leadership, referring to specific organizations. At best, they may be called organizational innovations, but mostly they are limited to organizational improvements. They belong to levels 3 and 4.

An engineering firm was the major supplier of machines and tools for a multinational. At a certain point the management became aware of two phenomena: although formally they stated in their strategy that they wanted to work for companies which did not belong to the group, in fact this choice was only used to level out production capacity. For this reason, the firm could not be successful in this market. Second, the engineers had a tradition to impose their technological 'solutions' on the group's factories. This was due to the monopolistic relation they had with them. A new director wanted to transform the firm and formulated a new strategy: there would be no difference in the treatment of the factories of the group and of those outside, and co-manufacturing with the customer should be the new business principle. He tried in vain to 'transform' his company. Only when he became aware that the changes in his company also implied major changes in the client factories could the new strategy become implemented. What he first thought to be a task for 3 years had to be spread over six. The rules of the game between supplier and client had to be redesigned and learned.

5.4.3 Control Information

Do we follow up the development of the meaning that the various stakeholders involved in the transformation process attribute to this process?

People involved in level 5 activities should constantly be aware of the congruency of the changes in which they are involved. The congruency of the vision of the future which they create is directly linked to the degree by which it is shared by its stakeholders. At most, every 6 months and at least every year they should monitor their understanding of the outside world in which they are involved and should take action, through communications and debates, to maintain the shared vision.

The scanning of annual reports of organizations is a worthwhile source of data. They show their commitment to innovation and change. It is not so much the accounting content of these reports which is important but the form, the illustrations, the headings which are expressions of how changing values are expressed. The medium is the message. And the propaganda, the communication to the outside world, is an indicator of the steering actions relevant for this level.

If various projects are going on at the same time for realizing a whole-system change, then a half-yearly or yearly debate between the project leaders can be a good indicator of the coherence between the projects. This coherence is directly related to the perceived congruence of the change.

In fact, process level 5 as the highest level in the innovation domain is also the lowest in the value-systems one and the examples are indicating already the political nature of the activities on this level. *By political nature I mean dealing with different, even contradictory, world views and value systems.* The control information on process level 5 is sensing these differences and the steering action is a balancing act to maintain coherence in this environment. This is completely different from the indicators used in the literature on innovation projects. Perhaps what is called the intuition of entrepreneurial innovators is much more rational than previously assumed. They are monitoring and interpreting signals of a different kind from those thought to belong to the 'rational' world, the world of figures and 'facts'.

5.4.4 Audit Information

How far do the stakeholders of an innovation still adhere to the values which were the basis of their decision to transform a whole system?

When at the end of these long-term projects we start to be confronted by winners and losers, by the expected and unexpected outcomes of our project, do we still recognize the values that were behind our choices? Are we still able to defend them before adversaries and friends alike? Debates in public forums give this audit information. We start to understand better how far or how near we are from our own value systems. Another rich but difficult source of audit data comes from reflecting why whole-system changes aborted or why important projects have been discontinued. As desirability and feasibility are clearly value judgements and the expression of underlying value systems, the understanding of 'failed' or 'successful' innovations alike helps the parties involved to assess the basis of the value judgements which led to the result.

The management of research and development divisions is often characterized by deep clefts between schools of thought. The same phenomenon can be found in highly professionalized work systems such as psychiatric hospitals or consulting firms. Because of the positivistic scientific ideology, indoctrinated during the academic training of the people involved, it is not often that the debate between schools of thought goes beyond a debate about true or false. When I am confronted in practice with these wars I like to introduce the concept of relevance instead of truth. Relevance is a value judgement, which is based on the specific *Weltanschauung* of an individual. The debate about the relevance of a certain school of thought helps professionals to relate to their own evaluation of the situation at hand, hence to their own value systems. This breaks through the value-free carapace which makes the debate a dialogue of the deaf. From true or false, the debate develops into right or wrong and ultimately to the contextual relevance of the theories in use.

Software development is very prone to 'ideological' debates. There are champions of data-oriented and of activity-based approaches. Operating systems, database philosophies, software language choices lead to Homeric debates. One of the means of sharpening the debate between the fighting parties is to confront them with the users of the systems to be developed. They become the context of the debate and oblige the champions to clarify in understandable language what the distinctions are. Often, emphatic distinctions between schools are then reduced to minor differences.

Ulrich[5] has a golden rule to deal with this kind of conflict: the debate of the relevance of an approach never can be held in the language of the approach. Expert and non-expert are both laypeople in the debate about relevance. When this debate has high quality, transferability and systemicity are improved.

5.4.5 Development Activities

These activities aim at whole-system transformations. In business terms this signifies the creation of whole new product/ service/market/technology combinations. In more general terms this results in the creation of a new network of relations between stakeholders who were previously unknown to each other, or whose relations were completely different.

These activities involve the creation of a new purpose and are always perceived with foresight or hindsight as *revolutions* by the relevant stakeholders. Life after such an innovation will never be the same again.

From the Napoleonic wars to the Gulf War, we have seen that major conflicts have required completely new means of warfare. Technological innovations have imposed strategic and tactical innovations. In his book Norman Dixon[6] correctly points out that preparation for the next war is always inadequate, because it is based upon the experiences of the previous one. Warfare has now arrived at a stage where the basic distinction between civilian and military has disappeared. All wars have become 'civil' wars: the military are better protected against military technology than civilians. The basic rationale for an army, as a provider of security for the non-military, has disappeared. Politicians are still trying to define new rules of a game which has changed its basic nature.

It is important to note that when projects are presented which have a time span of 5 to 10 years they will change the rules of the game in the area of the activities concerned, even if this is not stated formally.

Computers have often been introduced into the logistic processes of a business on the grounds that they would improve logistic efficiency: to reduce stocks, to speed up throughput time, to improve the follow-up of material and goods flow. Large projects have been set up: time horizons of 6 or 7 years for integrated projects are quite normal. Management was not aware that these projects would do more than improve efficiency, that they would change the nature of the business itself. Even if the concepts and the technologies used were adequate and of high quality, failures have abounded. Too little effort and attention has been given to the transferability and systemicity attributes of what in fact was an innovation. Relations between sales, planning, production, product engineering, purchasing and the customers needed to change fundamentally.

5.5 APPLICATIONS AND INTERVENTIONS IN THE INNOVATION DOMAIN

5.5.1 Some Thoughts on the Mission and the Management of Corporate Activities for Several Business Units

I use this text for 'kombinats' in Eastern and Central Europe, and also in Western companies, which are struggling with the consequences of restructuring their activities along business lines. Indeed, if the boundaries of a business unit have been correctly chosen, many 'corporate' activities, such as resource allocation, financial control or central services, change in nature. The basic idea behind the text is that corporate management, i.e. a superstructure above the work systems in the added-value domain, should only be concerned with innovative activities. In essence, the corporate centre forms project groups whose contributions are evaluated by the business units of the added-value domain. This is quite different from many activities at the corporate level in East and West alike. This text has the objective of sorting out activities and work systems in the overcomplex corporate structure, with all its specialist staff functions. It illustrates how the conceptual framework can be translated into common business terms. At first, the statements appear to be common practice. Nevertheless, dissociation of activities from the classically defined organizational structures leads to fundamental changes in the relations between corporate level and businesses, between the innovation domain and the added-value one.

5.5.1.1 Basic Principle

There is no need to create a superstructure above business units if this does not result in an added-value for them. As the business units are paying for corporate activities, they must be able to appreciate this added-value. For this reason, it is good to involve the business unit managers in corporate management in one way or another. But then they must be able to participate from two different perspectives: they are representatives of their own business unit and they are participants in the management of the synergy between the business units. They must learn to cope with the tension between these two perspectives and not only rely upon corporate management either as the one to blame or as the one on whom they depend completely in corporate matters. When corporations are very diversified it may happen that no synergy can be created between the different businesses. In this case, either corporate activities are a cost or a subtracted value or they belong to the value-systems domain (Chapter 6). In any case, the economic rationality which gives to corporations or holdings the role of the efficient allocation of resources appears to be a myth. The possession of power and control is also a myth. Corporations are work systems in their own right, and are unable to regulate the sum of the business units or divisions. The self-regulating nature of work systems and their autopoiesis places all power and control issues in the right context: these are self-defeating. Power and control are the Emperor's clothes that a child sees are not there.

An important public sector industry was privatized. Clearly, its activities belonged to three quite different businesses. Nevertheless, for political reasons, the three divisions were placed under a corporate head office. While I was working with the management of this head office and was using the concept of corporate added-value, we became painfully aware that they had no will to work on synergistic innovations. Hence, when I mentioned that as a consequence they could only have a temporary role, namely to make the divisions completely autonomous, we mutually terminated the assignment. Since then, a new corporate CEO has been appointed and the first thing he did was to bring people together from the various divisions to create new synergistic businesses. In the shortest possible time, the directors of the divisions were integrated into the corporate management team.

5.5.1.2 Work Domains

Added-value domain

These activities should be kept to a minimum and be continuously evaluated by the management of the business units. This minimum is achieved by making the business units as autonomous as possible. But autonomy also means responsibility. In the added-value domain the business units should be completely responsible for the activities which contribute to their primary processes. This means:

- Direct purchase and handling of the incoming goods
- Their own production and transformation processes
- Their stock of finished goods and the dispatching of those goods
- The direct sales and marketing activities for the goods and services related to the primary process
- The post-sale services related to these goods and services: invoicing, claims, guarantees, etc.
- The development of the goods and services which belong to their normal markets.

For reasons of economy of scale, it may be useful to think that certain services are kept together and paid for by the business units. In this case yearly contracts have to be made between business units and central services, which become small work systems on their own. These contracts may be revoked after a yearly evaluation if a business unit no longer profits from the economy of scale and can purchase the services more cheaply outside.

It is important that central services mean services that are provided to some or all business units. It does not mean that the people providing these services necessarily have to be located in some 'headquarters'. The contracts, not the location, define whether the services are central or not.

In the long run, economy of scale will never be a sufficient reason to keep these services inside corporate activities. Only those services which have a strategic importance for all the business units are worth keeping and developing inside the corporation. The others may be sold off or joint ventures with businesses, specialized in these services, can be made.

In the added-value domain I see, in general terms, central services provided in the following areas:

- Procurement services: this means long-term contractual relations with suppliers of strategic raw materials, eventually with customers who are buying goods from various business units at the same time. For those suppliers and customers, 'account-managers' should be appointed who have as their basic responsibility the management of these contracts.
- Technological infrastructure: this means strategic specialist skills, which contribute to several business units: e.g. process automation skills, CNC skills, special techniques related to the core activities of the various business units.
- Human resource services: these should be limited to the two highest management levels of the business units: the corporation and the central services. Moving managers of these levels around with a frequency of 3 to 7 years maintains coherence in a strongly decentralized company.
- Infrastructural services: this may imply telecommunication, energy and data-processing capabilities. Its major objective is to keep the various

systems compatible. On the other hand, for maintaining strategic external relations with unions, with customers, with the political and legal authorities, central services can be provided.

• Financial services: this may include the mobilization of investment capital through joint ventures, subsidies or tax incentives, capital creation, etc. It is essential that the strategic character of these services is defined.

The management of the central services has the following contributions:

• It contributes as staff specialists for the management of the corporation in the domains in which they are specialized.
• It manages their professionals and enables them to keep their specialism up to date, so that they have at least a comparable price/quality with other suppliers of this kind of service.
• It proposes innovations which may enhance the long-term future of the corporation and business units alike.
• It organizes the transfer of its knowledge and skills to people in the various business units, when adequate.

All central services should not have more than two levels: the manager with his or her specific task and the professionals. Managers should act as the *primus inter pares* of the professionals: they must be the best in their profession. 'Professional general managers' are not able to manage specialized professionals.

Innovation domain

The corporation contains all those activities which are creating new business units for the future. A business unit signifies a product/service/market/technology combination.

New business units may be created by recombining the skills and markets of the existing units or by setting up new ones through research and development or through joint ventures or acquisitions. These activities cover a period of at least 5 years to, at most, 10 years. To make these major changes and investments acceptable to the existing business units it is essential to link them to the mission of the corporation as a whole. We understand here as 'mission' the implicit or (better) explicit reason for the existence of the corporation and its subsidiaries, shared by the major stakeholders of the company: customers, suppliers, employees, financers, community and authorities. Enough time should be devoted by the corporation's management team in whatever form to checking the major decisions at corporate level and at business unit level in relation to this mission. The quality of the debate over the mission will determine the quality of the long-term innovations which are undertaken in the form of projects under the holding. In fact, the mission of the corporation is a statement of its values. Its elaboration belongs to the value-systems domain (Chapter 6).

Each corporate innovative project should have its own project manager. The management of the corporation initiates and terminates projects. The necessary funds for these projects must always be partially provided by the business units.

5.5.2 Minimal Specifications for Innovative Projects

I use the following text for helping clients to define activities in the innovation domain. Again, elements of the conceptual framework are translated into current business language. The four general attributes for innovative processes—desirability, feasibility, transferability and systemicity—are implicitly taken care of in the specifications.

5.5.2.1 Project Environment

An innovative project changes conditions for a defined work system. A work system is a concept for defining a coherent set of activities which have a common purpose shared by the different stakeholders who define it: clients of the output of the system, beneficiaries and potential victims, actors who are creating the conditions for performing the output, owners who can decide if this work system should continue or stop. These owners mostly become the sponsors of the project, those who want to provide the resources in people, time and money for it. An innovative project can create another purpose and define new clients, actors or owners for the work system or it can transform profoundly the processes by which the output of the work system is now created.

The work system which will be changed or eventually be created by the project can be defined by a list of its major stakeholders and the expected results for its stakeholders: both positive and negative. The list of these assumed expectations defines the political environment of the project. The more stakeholders expect a satisfying outcome from the project, the more politically feasible it becomes. In any case, the aims of the project should be communicated to these stakeholders.

5.5.2.2 Project Definition

Purpose

A project definition is the result of a thorough debate between the members of a project team who wish to be seen as the owners, the champions of the project. It is their major means of communicating the aims and purpose of the project to the external stakeholders, who will be influenced positively or negatively by their results. The project definition is the charter of the project. It should be written down on a minimal number of pages.

Components of the definition

A name. As we baptize a child with a name, so should a project be baptized. The name should express in some way the desirability and the attractiveness of the project. It should have some slogan-like and propagandistic characteristic but without exaggerating claims. The tendency to use acronyms or even number codes is a way of creating an *esprit de corps*, a conspirational mood in the project team itself, but it may deter the stakeholders of the project.

The name of the parents. The core members of the project group, that is, the group which takes responsibility for making the project a success, should sign the project nominally. Such a group has a maximum of nine members. They have to bear the uncertainty associated with every innovative project. That is the major reason why project teams never can stay anonymous. Departments never take any risk! Even if the project fails, the way the group worked at and through the failure may lead to a worthwhile experience for the project group members. These members have to be known by name, because they form the interface of the project with its environment. A project leader should be named. He or she is accountable for the resources allocated to the project and to its sponsors. A project leader should have his or her own contribution in the project and should not only manage it. One should avoid having people in a project group who only have a representative role, i.e. who cannot commit themselves to project decisions without referring to a constituency or backbenchers. A project group may decide to ask for temporary contributions from people not belonging to the core group.

The purpose of the project. At the beginning of the project it is impossible to determine what it will be and how it will take its course. A way has to be found by walking, learning by doing. For this reason it is impossible to describe a project beforehand.

Nevertheless, behind each project there is an idea. Its reason and purpose can be stated by writing or visualizing both the following situations:

- Describe the context and the work system in which the project positions itself when the project has been successfully completed. What will be the

innovative changes with which the various stakeholders will be confronted?
• Describe the context and the work system at which the project is if the project does not take place. What are the changes with which the various stakeholders will then be confronted?

The time horizon of the project. The time between the definition of the project and the moment when the project is intended to be operational, i.e. when its results are taken for granted and can be achieved in a routine way, we call the time horizon for the project. An innovative project will require at least 2 years and at most 10 years. This time should be part of the definition of the project. It determines the frequency for reporting and control relevant for that project: this should be approximately after each 10% of the total time. This also determines the time which may be devoted for diverging activities, scanning alternatives, experimenting with different approaches, etc. This time should occupy at most 20% of the total time and use at most 20% of available resources. This relation is a rule of thumb, which defines the efforts that will be devoted to the 'divergent' phase of the project. Divergent activities cannot be steered by means of the desired ends, only the means can be monitored. After 20% of the time span, a clear decision should be taken whether the project should be continued or stopped. Stopping a project is as skilful an art in project management as is completing it successfully. Once the decision has been taken to complete a project, the steering parameter becomes the desired outcome of the project, while the means are seen only as constraints. As has become clear, the time horizon defines the nature of the innovation.

The upper threshold of the resources needed. The project definition should contain the permitted resources in money, person-months or other expense parameters. These resources must be seen as an upper limit, which permits the sponsors and the project leader to determine what resources are still available, instead of having to focus on what has already been spent. The resources are also the result of negotiation between the project leader and the group and the sponsors, i.e. those who are providing the means. They define the ambition level of the project and are an indicator of its feasibility.

Other related projects. To ensure the systemicity of the project it is essential to make an inventory of any other known project focusing on the same domain, context and work system as the project defined. The interfaces with other projects will have to be managed by what is called a steering committee, which consists of the sponsors of the projects on the inventory.

This steering committee, which in fact cannot be anything other than an advisory committee of the major stakeholders, is a political forum where the quality attributes of the project can be monitored. This committee can be a large group.

The project leaders of the various projects should meet regularly and eventually decide to combine projects or to create a new one, which comes from the synergy between existing projects.

The legal and environmental constraints. No projects are undertaken in an administrative vacuum: they are carried out within legal constraints and have to take certain environmental constraints for granted. It is worth exploring these constraints and mentioning explicitly those which seem to be relevant for the sponsor and other stakeholders of the project.

REFERENCES

1. Ackoff, R. (1981). *Creating the Corporate Future*, Wiley
2. McLuhan, M. (1962). *The Gutenberg Galaxy: the Making of Typographic Man*, University of Toronto Press
3. Kuhn, T. (1970). *The Structure of Scientific Revolutions*, University of Chicago Press
4. Hoebeke, L. (1994). *Over boundaries: a theory for people at work*, Kunst en Projekten, Zedelgem, Belgium
5. Ulrich, H. and Probst G.J.B. (1984). *Self-organization and Management of Social Systems*, Springer-Verlag, Berlin
6. Dixon, N. (1979). *On the Psychology of Military Incompetence*, Futura

Chapter 6

—————— The Third Recursion Level:
the Value-systems Domain

6.1 BASIC DESCRIPTION OF THE DOMAIN

Here we come into the domain where our conceptual division between a set of activities and one of relations becomes less relevant. Already at the last process level of the innovation domain, the personal relations with stakeholders are essential for the transfer of innovative ideas. Support cannot be obtained anonymously: innovations are always linked to faces.

In the value-systems domain, *from a time span of more than 5 years*, if we include the last process level of the innovation domain *until a time span of 50 years* the major process is the creation of a new value language through an ongoing debate. This language is the substrate within which the innovations of the previous domain can be discovered and introduced. Although the process and its outcome may appear abstract, its reality resides in the persons participating in the construction of the new values.

Writing a book like this therefore creates a specific paradox. Its ambition is to invent a new language to use for the many facets of organized human work. But it can only employ an existing language for that purpose. The concepts developed in it can only become alive and show their relevance through debates, because it is itself the result of many debates. In Chapter 8, which is my trial and possibly error for starting debates, I try to draw some controversial consequences of the previous chapters, which may look like *déjà vu*. Although in our culture the written word is accepted as the most adequate medium to transfer language and values, it has many shortcomings in relation to the process which creates new values: debate.

A description of the generic process which belongs to the value-systems domain is as follows.

The value-systems domain is involved in the permanent creation of the elements of a new culture by creating new languages and new descriptions and prescriptions about the world through a permanent debate between carriers of different world views, traditions and cultures.

In fact, the activities belonging to the value-systems domain could be called political. But the word 'political' has been used in so many different ways that a more stringent definition is needed. *Political activities refer to interactions between proponents of different value systems not to achieve a certain form of consensus or compromise but to agree that it is worth continuing the debate and its underlying relations.* The author who has best described this dimension is Geoffrey Vickers[1]. As a civil servant and as chairman of the then National Coal Board in the UK he had, as a reflective practitioner, been able to convey the essentials of political transactions or of the activities belonging to the value-systems domain. He coined the terms 'appreciative systems', which refers to the system of values various stakeholders have and 'mutually satisfactory relations', which point to the maintenance of the relations as the desired outcome of the debate between the exponents of different appreciative systems. The negative connotation that the word 'political' has had in most American management literature is perhaps due to its focus upon the added-value domain and its bias towards results. From this perspective it is impossible to understand the intrinsic value of political processes inside or outside organizations.

As in the previous domains, some attributes of the process and its output can be given. In the value-systems domain process and output cannot meaningfully be distinguished. The debates are continuing and do not lead to a well-defined output. In terms of Vickers[1] and Checkland[2], appreciative systems tap continuously into the intertwined strands of ongoing events and ideas to feed the debate. Thus no decisions are taken in the value-systems domain, neither are there visible outputs. If there are any, they have to be seen as innovations.

The Constitution or the Bill of Rights, which was written down by the founding-fathers of the United States, was a result of an ongoing debate between Jefferson, Franklin, Washington and others. The Bill in itself was an innovation: it defined the rules of the game for a new kind of governance. In fact, Constitutional Courts can be seen as forums for the ongoing debate. The paradox with which they are confronted is that the debate has to be held within the confines of the existing Constitution. The Institution itself is an innovation generated by the value system behind the Constitution.

The following attributes are thus generic for the process and the outcomes of the activities, which belong to the value-systems domain. It is inevitable that these attributes are strongly coloured by my own value system. Perhaps this is the reason why I refer more here than in other chapters to various authors with whom I share certain values. They may be seen as members of the platform where the ongoing debate about human work is taking place. I do not quote them as 'external' authorities about whose values I wish to elaborate. Their views have influenced mine and I express my understanding of their world view. They are partners in my external and internal dialogue.

6.1.1 Generative

Suresh Srivastva and David Cooperrider[3] coined the term 'generative theories' in social sciences. They compare them with explicative theories. *Generative theories empower their users to develop a new repertoire of behaviour, of ways to deal with their natural and cultural environment.* Explicative theories can be seen more as constraining this repertoire between the confines, which are determined by the scientist-expert, who expresses his or her intentions in 'deterministic' laws. In fact, as Habermas[4] and others have pointed out, all language is intentional and thus generative of behaviour. Language is doing and doing is language: this is surely a daily experience for every human being. Maturana and Varela[5] even extrapolate this idea for all living beings. Hence, new languages are creating new behaviours and vice versa. We will find in Chapter 7 that in the spiritual domain, behaviour becomes the most important language and generates, in turn, new languages.

During the Second World War, Belgian employers and union representatives met each other in German prison camps and started to appreciate through debate their respective world views. The development after the war of the rules of the game of what has been called a mixed economy can be seen as the result of these debates.

The concepts developed in this book have been conveyed to many management teams in all kinds of organizations. I like to point out to the members of these teams that I provide them with a basic vocabulary and some rules of grammar, so that they can start to write their own poems and stories.

In the same vein, Soft Systems Methodology provides some basic grammar, like the elements of the CATWOE mnemonic for defining root definitions of work systems, which has generated hundreds of different root definitions, relevant for taking action in problematic issues. The emphasis of Checkland upon debate, while using SSM, is an indication that SSM in itself is an innovation which bridges the gap between the value-systems domain and the innovation one. The debate that SSM generates in systems journals is indicative of the same position.

6.1.2 Tolerant

The quality of a debate and its outcome are directly related to the tolerance of its members for different cultures, languages and world views. A greater diversity of world views makes more new synergistic connections possible which will lead to genuinely generative debates. The consciousness that the participants in the debate have to live together with its results is a valid although negative incentive for tolerance. A major distinction has to be made between tolerance and acceptance. *Tolerance means that although I cannot agree with certain world views or values, I do not judge their proponents or try to eliminate them. Acceptance means that I no longer make an effort to change a state of affairs which goes directly against my world view and values.* Acceptance is an expression of political powerlessness, tolerance presupposes that the relation between political adversaries is an essential element to express my values in new ways of behaving.

Too often in parliamentary democracies representatives are forced to become intolerant when they are reduced to becoming spokesmen for constituencies. Reducing the democratical debate to a vote of a numerical majority against a numerical minority leads to political inertia. Ironically the French say: 'plus ça change, plus c'est la même chose', and a slogan in a presidential campaign was ' la continuité dans le changement'. In working democracies members of the majority are aware that their relation with the members of the minority is primordial for the functioning of a democratic system. Unhappily, spokesmen seem to be unable to express this necessity publicly and this can be seen as the basis for alternate world views in government. Voters do not change their world view or value systems with each 'electoral landslide'. They use the only means at their disposal to emphasize the importance of the continuity of the relations between opposite world views.

6.1.3 Dialectical

Tolerance does not mean working towards a unifying common denominator, towards a general consensus, towards a grey compromise. A good debate is held by tolerant adversaries who increase the quality of the debate by testing their own world view by means of the other view. Adversaries reveal their own value systems to each other by challenging them seriously. It is useful to point out the difference that Peter Block.[6] made between enemies and adversaries in his *The Empowered Manager*.

Adversaries have a trusting relation. Although their values and world views may be completely contradictory, nevertheless they appreciate and trust each other as human beings. The best metaphor for adversarial relations comes from sport. In chess, tennis or football, the quality of the game is enhanced when both parties are competent and convinced of their success. During the game, they put all their effort against each other but at the same time they appreciate their adversary. The competition enhances their creativity within the constraints of the rules of the game.

Enemy relations lack this trust. In fact as René Girard[7] has pointed out, an enemy becomes the reification of the projections of the dark side, the 'evilness' of someone. Fighting an enemy is essentially self-destructive, because the fight is directed against what one cannot tolerate in oneself. Rightly, Block notes that all effort spent against an enemy backfires against oneself. Jerry Harvey ironically refers to the discovery of his own fingerprints on the knife which stabbed him in the back. The dialectical relation between adversaries breaks down into two warring factions which ultimately destroy each other as exemplified in many mythical and actual fights.

When I am confronted in an assignment with 'warfare' situations, i.e. those in which exponents of different value systems have stopped being on 'speaking' terms, my major efforts are not spent on 'peace making', but on the restoration of the dialectic relation. This may succeed after poorly assimilated mergers or acquisitions, or after traumatic events which have not been worked through. In former Communist countries, the rejection of the past and its reification in the older generation by the younger one is another example. The enmity which sometimes characterizes the relations between politicians and public servants is a third example. A history of 'poor' industrial relations can also create a cold war environment. One of the questions which helps the two parties to rediscover their common ground is what they should do if the other party no longer existed. This obliges the members of one faction to start to consider the operationalization of their own values instead of being obsessed by the impossibilities generated by the 'enemy'.

6.1.4 Congruent

Debates are not detached discussions 'about' something. *Persons taking part in debates which create new value systems are personally involved and have the difficult task of recreating their own world views. If they are not thoroughly grounded in their own humanity and its traditions, if they have not creatively integrated these traditions in their own lives, they risk their own personality in the debate. The debate requires and strengthens the congruency between the inner and outer worlds of the participants.*

Again, much of what is called public debate is very far from what I call debate in the value-systems domain. When people are obliged to behave as spokepersons for constituencies, which in fact are pure social constructions, the probability of self-censorship increases. Only those elements are brought into the debate which reinforce the existing standpoints, irrespective of the personal values of the representative. Political credibility is much more linked to congruency than to ideological stubborness. Many young people, who started full of idealistic expectations and were militant for values in organized settings, leave the organization in disillusion, or become cynical 'political' animals. The setting in which they began is not conducive to personal congruency. The right time perspective for debates in the value-system domain is shortened drastically when winning elections becomes the first objective. Elections should rather be seen as part of the information control system for activities in the value-systems domain, not ends in themselves. Influential politicians always have a long-term perspective and are not worried by short-term electoral concerns. Although their values do not change quickly, they learn through ongoing debates more about themselves and their relation with their own values through good and bad political times.

Although the political domain in our Western democracies is one of the important forums for the value-systems domain, it is not limited to it. In the same way that innovation cannot be identified with technological innovations, debates in the value-systems domain are not limited to the formal political domain. In all domains of human endeavour new value systems are continuously created.

The IASA in Laxenburg, Austria, has been a place where system scientists from West and East have met to develop a systems language which transcends the ideological contradictions between what was called the free world and the Communist bloc. In the same vein, the Pugwash conferences were created by scientists concerned about the military use of nuclear science. They have been instrumental in the nuclear weapons treaties between the USA and the former USSR.

The previous examples indicate that in the value-systems domain we leave the world of organizations and start to work with associations: these are groups of persons who are involved in the activities belonging to the domain for only part of their working life and who freely join these associations. Here I follow the terminology of Jaques[8], who makes a difference between organizations that employ and pay people, which he calls bureaucracies, and associations, which are different in nature. One of the consequences is that activities in the value-systems domain are always interorganizational. People involved in these activities belong to one or other organization and freely join associations where the debates of the value-systems domain are taking place. Referent organizations (see further in Section 6.3), think tanks, are or could be forms for creating the value systems of the future (Figure 6.1). The large group (see Section 2.4) is the most adequate setting for associations developing new values and languages.

6.2 PROCESS LEVEL 5: FROM 5 TO 10 YEARS

As between the added-value and the innovation domains, we find a common process level in the innovation and the value-systems domains. Whole-system innovations are expressions of the values developed in the value-systems domain but are, at the same time, essential contributions to the ongoing debates in the creation of new values. Here also we can reformulate the basic strategic dilemma which belongs to this level.

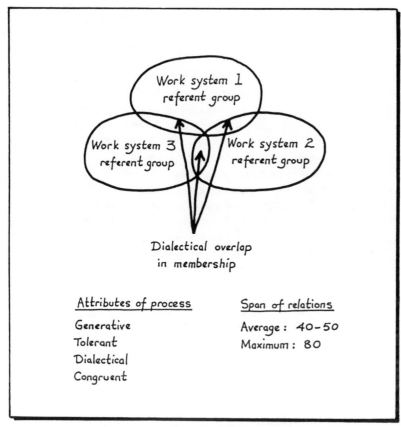

Figure 6.1   The value-systems domain

Basic strategic dilemma: a whole-system innovation creates a bifurcation point, a point of no return. Through the assessment of the consequences of the innovation the value system behind it is challenged. The innovation implies the change of the innovator. He or she can accept or reject the 'parenthood' of the innovation.

After Hiroshima and Nagasaki, the scientists who developed nuclear technology reacted very differently. All had been touched in their personal values. But not all of them were able to work through the event. One of the mechanisms to avoid the working through was splitting: we made the bomb, but it was the responsibility of the government to use it against Japan.

I see the same kind of discourse used by the proponents of 'shock therapy' in former Communist countries. Creating a 'free market' in a planned economy has never been done before. The economic shock therapy is as good a gamble as anything else. But when things are going awry it does not help to blame the politicians as do some economic advisors. Economic shock therapy cannot be divided into a political and an economic component: it is political economy, as well as economic politics.

The consequences of innovations are the ultimate test for the values which generated them in the first place, in the same way that the 'market place' is the ultimate test for the success of an innovation. But success or failure in the marketplace has not such a profound personal impact on the innovators as the working through of the good and bad consequences of an irreversible innovation, related to their own values. In Chapter 7 we will see how this kind of experience is related to the spiritual domain.

If innovations, mainly technological ones, are perceived only as the consequences of the value-free pursuit of knowledge and truth, without challenging the values behind this value freedom, people and groups in society will take up this ethical challenge in a self-regulating way. This is perhaps one of the major reasons why at the end of this century the scientific ethos becomes increasingly under attack.

The search for the origins of and a cure for the current AIDS epidemic is already being conditioned by the lobbying of pressure groups. The value component can no longer be omitted. Scientific conferences on AIDS are surrounded by all kinds of political activities. This may be seen as a nuisance for the positivistic value-free scientists involved in research, or it may give them a strong signal that their relation towards the values of value-free science is challenged.

The lack of funding of what is called fundamental research by most governments can also be considered as a self-regulating mechanism which challenges the values behind the classical scientific approaches. Value-free technological assessment methodologies will not help to curb the trend of diminishing funds.

Again, I have to stress that it is impossible for me to write about activities in the value-systems domain without declaring the values behind my writing. I hope that the previous statements and the following paragraphs may be read in this way and may lead to useful debate. In this way, the title of this book: *Making Work Systems Better*, can also become meaningful in the value-systems domain.

6.3 PROCESS LEVEL 6: FROM 10 TO 20 YEARS

6.3.1. Generic Transformation Process

In a given area of human activities, members of referent groups debate their 'appreciative systems' and thus create a coherent language about their area for stimulating activities in the innovation domain.

This sentence needs some explanation. A given area of human activity can be seen as an area in which whole system changes have a meaning. For example, we can speak of the health sector, regional development, economic or political disaster areas, scientific sectors, etc. There is always something arbitrary in the delineation of areas of human activity. In fact, as with all system definitions, the definition of an area of human activities is also a choice based upon the intentions and the constraints of the persons for which this choice is relevant.

A multidisciplinary group has started debates at the University of Santa Fé, USA, and has taken as its area of activities the understanding of all kinds of non-linear behaviour. Their 'appreciative system' is that the creation of a qualitative language (mathematical or not) may shed a new light upon phenomena, which are of concern at the end of this century: economic and financial issues, conflicts, ecology, climatic changes, etc. The debates in the group struggle with the paradox of using a deterministic language for discussing non-deterministic phenomena.

A referent group is a concept documented by Eric Trist[9], after he started to bring together in what are called search conferences the representatives of the major stakeholders of de-industrialized areas of Pennsylvania, USA. The conferences had no decision-taking power at all: the representatives listened to and debated carefully with each other. On their return to their constituencies, their own organizations, they started to perform innovations influenced by what they knew to be valued by the other members, even if these were in contradiction to their own aims and values.

The way global strategies are devised in Japan runs parallel to the concept of referent groups. Political, business , union and financial leaders meet to 'drink tea', as it is called. They listen to each other and return to their organizations, pursuing their own aims but knowing that these can only be achieved when they maintain mutually satisfactory relations with the other parties involved. The coherence of Japanese industrial policy is not based upon elaborate plans and decisions but upon a genuine feeling for the various 'appreciative' or value systems in hand and a tendency to maintain mutually satisfactory relations.

The work of Geoffrey Vickers is essential for understanding the activities in the value-systems domain. His experience as a civil servant and as chairman of the former National Coal Board was, for him, a basis for reflecting and for creating relevant concepts for what may be called the real political domain: the domain where different value systems meet and are debated. The representatives of the various values know that they have to maintain their mutual relationship, even when these values contradict each other. If this fails, ideology takes over with the restrictive and oppressive powers that are unleashed when diversity is jeopardized.

The concept appreciative system is very near to what Checkland[10] calls

Weltanschauung. The delimitation of an area of activities is strongly dependent upon the *Weltanschauung* of the various members of the debate. When working with root definitions in the value-systems domain, their most important components are the *'Weltanschauung'* and 'Environmental Constraints' as expressions of the various *Weltanschauungs*. The quality of the debates in the value-systems domain is directly related to the capacity of the members of referent groups to explore the boundaries of their personal relation with their values by meeting the boundaries of other members.

The reorganization of a mental health hospital became a stalemate when two contradictory *Weltanschauungs*, represented by two psychiatric 'schools', could not come to terms. One school defined the primary process as the healing of patients through the intervention of therapists and psychiatrists, while the other school defined it as the creation of physical and psychological conditions in which patients could heal themselves. It appeared impossible to redefine the boundaries of the system by means of a selection process, in which the relevance of each approach for a given patient could be assessed.

The previous example teaches us two more elements of activities in the value-systems domain:

- When value-system debates are going on within the confines of organizational boundaries, difficulties are bound to occur. The issues with which the two psychiatric schools were struggling are broader than the context of a reorganization. The 'unmanageability' of organizations with a preponderance of highly professional people can be seen in the light of a confusing of the various domains: the added-value domain, where organizational issues are relevant, the innovation domain, where projects and project work is relevant, and the value-systems domain, where an ongoing debate is relevant. These debates need a broader forum than one organization. In fact, both psychiatric schools received their impetus from professional forums, which had not come to terms with the basic strategic dilemma belonging to process level 6. As Jaques[8] points out, associations are more important platforms in process level 6 than organizations.
- The time span of the debates in process level 6 is 10 to 20 years. Pressure upon the members of the debate to produce short-term results or to take short-term decisions is essentially counterproductive. One of the ways in which the stalemate between the two psychiatric schools could have been overcome was to start innovative pilot projects for exploring the boundaries between the two schools. Prestructuring the outcome of the debate, instead of solving the conflict, exacerbates it. In this case, the economic rationality of the reorganization, typical of the added-value domain, created a self-defeating mechanism.

6.3.2. Basic Strategic Dilemma

The creation of new value systems and languages is 'abstract' and has an 'idealistic' flavour. The tension between ideology and value systems is continuously present.

For this reason, the basic strategic tension on this level is to avoid as much as possible the 'division' between good and evil. As all value systems are artificial, but contain an implicit intention to create a better world, the people who embody them are always tempted to split off the adverse consequences: evil is performed by those who criticize their value system. Then ideology is lurking: people are neither angels nor beasts. He who wants to behave like an angel behaves like a beast, wrote Pascal[11].

A specific form of working with referent groups has been designed by Stafford Beer and used in, for example, Pacific Bell[12]. Beer uses the word 'Tensegrity' and employs as an analogy the geodesic constructions of Buckminster Fuller, in which contradictory tensions between the various elements of the structure are a guarantee of its extreme coherence and structural stability. Beer's structuring of the debate creates conditions for dealing with the strategic dilemma on this level. The dialectical role that each member of the debate has in two different subgroups helps them to avoid splitting.

Another way to help referent groups to deal with the basic strategic dilemma is shown by the four quadrants in Figure 6.2. The vertical axis shows the dimension from concrete to abstract. Concrete language refers to personal experiences, to anecdotic evidence, to accepted measurements, etc. Abstract language constructs common patterns from a series of events and experiences. A 'table' is an abstraction of many experiences with activities and behaviour for which tables were an essential component.

The horizontal axis in Figure 6.2 shows the dimension from specific to general. The more general a statement, the more it sounds context-free. The more specific a statement, the more it has to be understood in a specific context. General statements have a slogan-like quality and when they are recognized easily lead to jokes. 'Ideological utterances' belong to the general and abstract category.

In former Communist countries the following joke is circulating: Capitalism is the exploitation of men by men, while Communism is just the opposite.

Specific statements always refer to the context of the person who expresses them. When Maturana and Varela[5] say that everything said is said by someone, they make a general statement about the specificity of language as action.

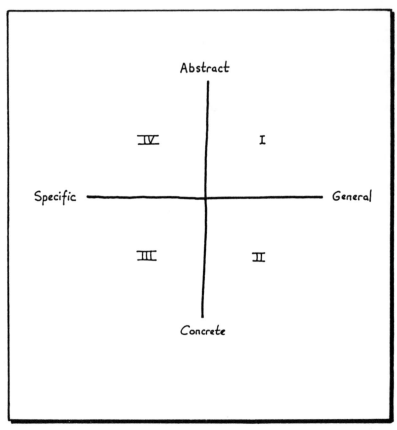

Figure 6.2 A quadrant for statements of the debates in the value-systems domain

To help members of referent groups to enhance the quality of the value-systems debates in which they participate, I ask them to position their major statements into the four quadrants, formed by the two axes. The most difficult transition is from quadrant I (general and abstract) to quadrant IV (specific and abstract). Nevertheless, statements which belong to the fourth quadrant for the debaters are the richest and lead to innovative thinking and action. When the referent group is ideologically conflict-ridden, one of the ways to overcome stalemates is to start from quadrant III (specific and concrete). Each member starts to tell anecdotes from personal experience, which is significant for his or her *Weltanschauung* and which expresses how the present conflicts have been painfully experienced. In this way value systems are related to the persons: the relations between values and persons become visible in the group and lead to the development of relations between its members. Every member in his or her own way has been the victim of specific value systems. This is the basis for adversarial emotions in the group.

The 'broadcasting' media create images, which belong to quadrant II. Very concrete images are separated from their specific context and in this way receive 'universal' characteristics. Greenpeace is one of the multinational organizations which has discovered the political value of this transformation process. (See Chapter 8: controversy 6).

6.3.3 Control Information

When referent groups are able to manage their membership in terms of the relevance of the debate they are self-regulated. Membership assessment should be undertaken at least every two years or, more frequently, annually to provide steering information.

It is typical of mature groups that they are able to deal regularly with departures and with newcomers. Once it becomes difficult to find new participants for the referent group, a strong signal is given that it is losing its relevance.

Modernist and progressive ideologies have always emphasized the importance of the creation of new languages, perspectives and stressed innovations. But, as we have seen, these activities have their own time dimension and cannot be accelerated. A mature referent group needs time to form and to perform. Progressive platforms of debate have a self-regulating but also self-defeating tendency to break up. Ideological struggles lead to the formation of schools, sects or factions. Dialectical relations are broken and internecine war starts. Dialectical and generative capabilities only work in the context of tolerance and congruence. The four attributes are, at the same time, a result and a condition for referent groups working in the value-systems domain.

When I mentioned that in the innovation domain the concept of failure or success is not relevant for convinced and able innovators because the probability of success is rather low, the requirements of tolerance and congruence in referent groups limits even more the number of people interested in continuous long-term debate. It is therefore quite natural that few of them have a long history. Indeed, this is happily so: social systems can cope only slowly with new world views and languages. Too many of them could be disruptive, as has been shown repeatedly in so-called revolutions. The fact that the creators of the new language and world view have themselves to cope with this disruption in their own persons and in the membership of their referent groups is the best self-regulating guarantee for their efforts.

In my own experience it has been extremely difficult to create or to be a member of a referent group, consisting of representatives of different tendencies, which could refrain from taking decisions or actions as a group. This has been the case for advisory boards of professional or political associations.

It could be worth reviewing the history of psychiatry from Freud onwards in the light of its referent groups and their subsequent breaking up.

In the same way, we can look at the history of Marxism and its various expressions. It is paradoxical that the continuity of Marxism, which tried to operationalize dialectics in practice, has been embodied in parties and regimes where dialectics were banned. Here also, history could be reviewed in terms of the lack of tolerance and congruence in the members of the groups representative of the development of the Marxist world view.

6.3.4 Audit Information

The way the referent groups are spoken of in the innovation and added-value domains, the respect they deserve is the major warning to avoid the fate of many of them: to become an 'old boy's network', whose members seem to have lost touch with their own environment.

The quality of the selection of members of the associations which create value systems as their task is of paramount importance. Inbreeding is one of their major pitfalls. Exclusion of dissenters is a corollary of inbreeding. Once the dialectics are gone, the association not only becomes sterile but it also has a great likelihood of becoming harmful. Public appreciation, which does not mean plebiscites only, is a signal to be taken into account. There is a sound public distrust of poorly functioning associations involved in creating value systems.

People in charge of their profession's code of conduct quickly become defenders of its prerogatives once they can easily exclude dissenting members.

All kinds of regulatory bodies, from the certification of the ISO 9000 quality standard to what is called the legislative body in parliamentary democracies, have to struggle to maintain the dialogue. The greatest failure of these bodies is that they foreclose the generative aspects of high-quality expressions of value systems. A poor law or regulation stays a poor law or regulation, even if it is enforced. Enforcement only undermines the credibility of the regulating body. Audits in the value-systems domain should focus upon this credibility. It is the strongest signal that the expression of the new values in laws and regulations is in touch with the implicit values of those subjected to them. Referent organizations should contain representatives who are in real touch with their constituencies. These should not be seen as statistical aggregates, subject to all kinds of opinion polls, but as real people.

At the beginning of the first oil crisis the Netherlands government asked drivers to limit their speed to 100 km/h to save fuel. Police audits showed that this advice was followed by the majority. Later, when driving at more than 100 km/h became a transgression of the law and could lead to heavy penalties, the self-discipline of the Dutch drivers diminished. Enforcement is not a surrogate for meaningful behaviour. People who have driven a car for 20 years and more have learnt prudence as a value.

6.3.5 Development Activities

On this process level development becomes non-teleological.

The activities developed on this level do not have specific objectives, strategies or aims. Their only purpose is to maintain mutually satisfactory relations by a permanent debate between the different teleological visions, world views and perspectives of the members involved in this work. Some members are concerned with innovations, which are expressions of the state of the debate and which, in turn, feed that debate.

This may appear to be rather simple. Even the concept of a work system may look farfetched in these circumstances. In fact, developments in the value-systems domain illustrate the concept of recursion level very well. The activities on each recursion level have their own organizational closure and characteristics, which are different in nature from the other recursion levels. They have their own viability. Once in the value-systems domain, we leave the domain where results, aims, objectives, strategies are relevant.

This does not mean that people involved in these activities and in the development of new languages and values only meet and talk to each other. Direct contributions in the value-systems domain are not full-time activities. This is self-evident when one takes their time span into account. As the tale of the stonemasons (see Section 3.2) illustrated metaphorically, what one does is not an indication of the domain in which one is working. The perspective of one's actions makes them part of the ongoing debate: scientists may work in their laboratories, but this work is not aimed at solving problems, not even at discovering or inventing; managers may take up their management tasks but these are not directed directly at the success of their business or the creation of new businesses; union leaders or leaders of other pressure groups may be involved in industrial or political action, but their aim is not to change the state of affairs as soon as possible. The perspective of all of them is to maintain through their actions and experiences the feedback loop between their internal and external worlds and to check the languages and values which they help to develop.

Yearly or two-yearly conferences of 'learned associations' are for some people the platform on which they meet each other to take up the ongoing development of new world views and value systems.

When search conferences effectively contribute to the development of new value systems their members almost invariably plan follow-up sessions with an adequate frequency.

The role of the sessions of the Royal Society in England during the seventeenth to nineteenth centuries contributed to shaping scientific methodology not only in England but also in the rest of the Western world.

6.4 PROCESS LEVEL 7: FROM 20 TO 50 YEARS

6.4.1 Generic Transformation Process

On this process level a language and values are developed which encompass many areas of human activity. Cultures are also developed.

The value language of the Enlightenment made intensive use of the philosophical, scientific, ethical and political ideas of its time. It was able to create a coherent world view, which generated a combined creativity regarding the whole cultural sphere. Science and technology, economics and politics, institutional innovation and geographic exploration contributed coherently to create modern industrial states. *Post facto,* Jules Verne had written the parables of the Enlightenment. Modernism as a culture became established. Lavoisier and Franklin, Mozart, Adam Smith and many others were associated with the freemasons, one of the most important associations which created the new value system of the Enlightenment.

Here, I must introduce the social construct of culture. *A culture can be defined as a broad aggregation of people who share the same 'appreciative system', the same value language.* The relation between culture and language has long been accepted as self-evident. Habermas[13] sees language as 'communicative action', thus essentially intentional and hence value-laden. People belong to the same culture when they have more or less the same way of interpreting the ongoing stream of events and ideas (Vickers), and more or less the same way of translating their interpretation into action. I prefer not to fall into the ontological trap of using culture to represent something in the real world. Much more, culture is for me a construct which can be used relevantly in the context of shared value systems. The definition I use can be seen as a minimal critical specification.

The connection between ethnic language and culture is meaningful only when its members share similar behaviour. This is best exemplified by common rituals, which are based on a shared history, expressed in myths, stories and shared rationalizations.

Even though I read and write in English I do not belong to the English culture. My use of English as a vernacular is due to the fact that I belong to the aggregate of Western international system writers and practitioners. I have to share the review and marketing rituals to be accepted by a publisher recognized in the field.

Due to the time span of this process, the way in which development activities on this level are done can only be inferred with hindsight. Nevertheless, the actors in the process are well aware that they are at the root of important developments. They know each other, debate fiercely with one another and fight equally fiercely against the Establishment, as it is understood by them. Culture and counterculture are dialectically related.

In the same way, our Western intellectual culture is confronted with the results of the relativism which started to appear generally in art and science, politics and economics, anthropology, linguistics and history on the demise of the absolutist ideologies following the Second World War. What is now generally referred to as postmodernism finds its roots in individuals in the first half of the century such as Einstein and Picasso, Gödel and Stravinsky, Joyce and Duchamp. The values behind their works became widespread after the Second World War.

One interesting association to consider may be the group around Gregory Bateson. Stafford Beer and Ivan Illich, Watzlawick and Anthony Wilden, René Girard and Maturana, all of them referring to G. Bateson. All introduce an epistemological and systemic stance into their value systems.

6.4.2 Basic Strategic Dilemma

The development of a new culture is bound to use the existing language of the 'Establishment'. Nevertheless, it changes the context of its usage. The tension between rupture and displacement has to be managed.

The dilemma consists of not trying to throw out the baby with the bathwater. If the new value system has to lead to new kinds of behaviour and new widespread world views, there must be a possibility of anchoring it in the existing value systems.

The United Kingdom has moved faster towards the new values of the industrial state than France, because Enlightment ideas were wide-spread throughout France's former aristocracy. The French revolutionaries identified the old values with persons, who became victims of the Terror. The United States has been the most fruitful country for trying out the new values. The rejection of their colonial past created a rupture with the English feudal system, but relations with the English intellectual elite were maintained.

Successful value-system transformations are able to make the elements of the new values apparent in existing behaviour and ways of thinking.

They reshape the old traditions by pointing to their 'original' presence, which has mostly been hidden by many layers of superficial offshoots. They *recreate* old human traditions. This is different from a restoration of the old values. Usually the results of restorers is to create a very similar institution to the one they are fighting against: the efforts of restorers are spent in the added-value or innovation domains. Every Establishment, be it religious, political, cultural or scientific, is confronted from time to time by groups positioning themselves clearly in its tradition, while at the same time they are perceived as revolutionaries.

For the Catholic Church, the Lutheran and Calvinistic Reformation could easily be classified as revolutionary. Their value system was incompatible with the Catholic tradition. They were quickly excommunicated. Protestant fundamentalism rapidly led them to a new Churchlike behaviour: they started also to 'excommunicate'. Much more difficult for the Church Establishment has been the position of the Jesuits. By some they were perceived as recreating the values of the Church, even as the stronghold of the Counter-Reformation, by others they were perceived as revolutionaries. It was the genius of Ignatius of Loyola that he introduced into the Constitutions the necessary dialectical mechanisms to permit the order to maintain that ambiguity for about 200 years.

On process level 7 the terms 'control' and 'audit' information are breaking down. These mechanisms become so all-pervasive among the actors in the process that separating them conceptually is no longer meaningful. The quality of the processes belonging to this level is directly related to the embodiment of the four attributes belonging to the value-systems domain by the persons involved in them: creativity (generative), tolerance, congruency and dialectical ability.

6.5 APPLICATIONS AND INTERVENTIONS IN THE VALUE-SYSTEMS DOMAIN

6.5.1 Basic Principles of the Mondragon Co-operative Experience*

In 1939, after the Spanish Civil War, an Experience was started by five Basque pupils of the Technical School of Mondragon under the impetus of José Maria Arizmendiarrieta, a local priest. Operationally it was the creation of a small co-operative, but based upon a strong value system, which questioned the contradiction between the social and the economic realms and its expression in the adversarial relations between employers and workers, between capital and labour, to use the ideological jargon common during this period.

The Experience is still thriving and has developed into a system of about

---

* Reproduced by permission of Corporacion MCC – Azatza, S.A.

100 co-operatives with activities in the industrial, financial and distribution sectors. There are actually about 22 000 co-operators. One of the founders, Ormaechea, has written the history of the co-operative, and at the end of his book he refers to the charter of the Experience. This is the summary of 50 years of trial and error, of institutional, economic and technological innovations. The basic principles of Mondragon are the minimal critical specifications of its values. The Mondragon Experience and its basic principles are a clear example of work done in the value-systems domain and its relation with the innovation domain. [14]

6.5.1.1 Open Admission

The Mondragon Co-operative Experience declares itself open to all men and women who accept these Basic Principles and prove themselves professionally capable of carrying out the jobs available. Therefore to join the Experience, there shall be no discrimination on religious, political or ethical grounds, nor any due to gender. The only requirement shall be a respect for its internal constitution. Open admission is the main guiding principle in the activities and relations between people in co-operative development.

6.5.1.2 Democratic Organization

The Mondragon Co-operative Experience proclaims the basic equality of its worker-members with respect to their rights to be, to possess and to know, which implies the acceptance of a democratic organization of the company, specified in:

1. The primacy of the General Assembly, made up of all the members, which operates on the principle of 'one member, one vote'.
2. The democratic organization of the governing bodies, specifically the Governing Council, which is responsible to the General Assembly in respect of its management.
3. The collaboration with the management bodies designated to manage the company by delegation of the entire community. These bodies shall have sufficient authority to carry out their functions efficiently for the common good.

6.5.1.3 Sovereignty of Labour

The Mondragon Co-operative Experience considers that Labour is the principal factor for transforming nature, society and human beings themselves and therefore it:

1. Renounces the systematic contracting of salaried workers.
2. Gives labour total primacy in the organization of co-operatives.

3. Considers labour to be worthy, in essence, in the distribution of the wealth created.
4. Manifests its will to extend the options for work to all members of society.

6.5.1.4 The Instrumental and Subordinate Character of Capital

The Mondragon Co-operative Experience considers Capital to be an instrument, subordinate to Labour, necessary for business development, and worthy, therefore, of:

1. Remuneration, which is:
   • Just, in relation to the efforts implied in accumulating capital.
   • Adequate, to enable necessary resources to be provided.
   • Limited in its amount, by means of corresponding controls.
   • Not directly linked to the Profits made.
2. Availability subordinate to the continuity and development of the co-operative, without preventing the correct application of the principle of open admission.

6.5.1.5 Participatory Management

The Mondragon Co-operative Experience believes that the democratic character of the Co-operative is not limited to membership aspects, and that it also implies the progressive development of self-management and consequently of the participation of members in the sphere of business management which, in turn, requires:

1. The development of suitable mechanisms and channels for participation.
2. Freedom of information concerning the development of the basic management variables of the Co-operative.
3. The practice of methods of consultation and negotiation with worker-members and their social representatives in economic, organizational and labour decisions which concern or affect them.
4. The systematic application of social and professional training plans for members.
5. The establishment of internal promotion as the basic means of covering posts of greater professional responsibility.

6.5.1.6 Payment Solidarity

The Mondragon Co-operative Experience proclaims sufficient and solidary remuneration to be a basic principle in its management, expressed in the following terms:

1. Sufficient, in accordance with the possibilities of the Co-operative.
2. Solidarity, in the following specific spheres:
   - Internal. Materialized, among other aspects, in the existence of a differential, based on solidarity, in payment for work.
   - External. Materialized in the criteria that average internal payment levels are equivalent to those of salaried workers in surrounding areas, unless the wage policy in this area is obviously insufficient.

6.5.1.7 Co-operation between Co-operatives

The Mondragon Co-operative Experience considers that, as a specific application of solidarity and as a requirement for business efficiency, the principle of interco-operation should be evident:

1. Between individual Co-operatives, through the creation of Groupings which tend towards the establishment of a homogeneous socio-labour system, including the pooling of profits, the controlled transfer of worker-members and the search for potential synergies derived from their combined size.
2. Between Groupings, by means of the democratic constitution and management, for the common good, of support entities and bodies.
3. Between the Mondragon Co-operative Experience and other Basque co-operative organizations, in order to promote the Basque Co-operative Movement.
4. With other co-operative movements in Spain, Europe and the rest of the world, making agreements and setting up joint bodies aimed at stimulating development.

6.5.1.8 Social Transformation

The Mondragon Co-operative Experience manifests its desire for social transformation based on solidarity with that of other peoples, through its activities in the Basque Country in a process of expansion which will contribute to economic and social reconstruction and to the creation of a Basque society which is more free, just and expresses solidarity, by means of:

1. The investment of the greater part of the Net Profits obtained, earmarking a significant proportion to Funds of community nature, to enable the creation of new jobs in the co-operative system.
2. The support for community development initiatives, through the application of the Social Welfare Fund.

3. A Social Security policy coherent with the co-operative system, based on solidarity and responsibility.
4. Co-operation with other Basque institutions of an economic and social nature, especially those promoted by the Basque working class.
5. Collaboration towards the recovery of Basque as the national language and, in general, of elements characteristic of Basque culture.

6.5.1.9 Universality

The Mondragon Co-operative Experience, as an expression of its universality, proclaims its solidarity with all those working for economic democracy in the sphere of the 'Social Economy', championing the objectives of Peace, Justice and Development, which are essential features of International Co-operativism.

6.5.1.10 Education

The Mondragon Co-operative Experience manifests that to promote the implantation of these Principles it is essential that sufficient human and economic resources be provided for Education, in its various aspects:

1. Co-operative, for all members and especially those elected to office in the social bodies.
2. Professional, especially for members appointed to management bodies.
3. In general, of youth, to encourage the emergence of new co-operators, capable of consolidating and developing the Experience in the future.

Very specific in this 'Constitution' is the operationalization of the relation between Labour and Capital, the differentiation between a Democratic Organization and Participatory Management, the definition of a salary differential, which changed recently from 1 to 3 to 1 to 6 and the delicate balance between an outspoken Basque frame of reference and a political open-mindedness, stated in the Open Admission principle. As in all good Constitutions, dialectical elements have been built in.

6.5.2 Proposal for a Search Conference for Defining Projects for Regional Development

What follows is a transcription of a proposal to start up a referent organization, involved in the regional development in an East European country. The potential participants have been overwhelmed with all kinds of planning activity, which were never implemented. For this reason, they became very enthusiastic for the constitution of a referent organization. In the transcription, I have eliminated only the elements which could help to identify the region. This is an example of creating a setting to start work in the value-systems domain.

6.5.2.1 Background and Aims of the Proposal

In the meeting with the Chamber of Commerce of the area the method of the referent organizations to stimulate regional development was explained in general terms. I repeat here the major principles behind this approach:

- Representatives of the major stakeholders of the region are brought together: employers, bankers, financers, politicians and heads of the public service, union representatives and other relevant parties. A referent group should never exceed 81 members. Groups of 40 to 50 people are very common.
- The group as such has no decision power. It is not its responsibility to make elaborate plans, policies or strategies. In this way, the representatives in the group are not submitted to the pressure of being accountable for decisions to their constituencies or the organizations they represent.
- The group is a forum for open discussion and debate, for tapping the creativity of its members, where it must be possible to air ideas without immediate sanction from other interest groups. The debates should not be publicly reported: only the results of the debates which the group members themselves decide to bring into the open will be communicated to the outside world via the media or other means.
- When people even with contradictory aims feel no pressure to agree to a joint proposal, plan or strategy, they are enabled to listen attentively to one another and once they are back in their own constituency or organization, they are free to make decisions in accord with their own objectives. Nevertheless, experience has shown that, because they hear different, even contradictory, viewpoints, they start to take them into account in their own decision making.
- In this way the various development projects begin to show a certain coherence, although there is no formal development plan or project to be agreed upon by every member or, worse, to be voted on by majority rule. The latter usually leads to overcomplex compromises, which do not generate the necessary commitment to act.
- In the referent group, clusters can start to form which then discover joint interests and decide *ad hoc* to define development projects shared by the members of the cluster. These types of project are the expected outcome of the proposed search conference. Because all the other members share the knowledge of these projects and have understood their rationality, because of the fierce debates in their defence, a common priority pattern

starts to develop. This also greatly enhances the coherence of all the development activities in the area.

This proposal aims to start up a referent organization by means of a two-day search conference. The results of the conference can be evaluated through:

- The quality of the project proposals, which will be defined during the conference. From 5 to 10 projects will already have been operationally defined or an action plan set up to reach a workable definition by the members of an interested cluster.
- The number of *ad hoc* shared informal problem-solving efforts which will emerge from the shared information.
- The willingness of the members of the referent group to continue their efforts and the time schedule for subsequent conferences.

6.5.2.2 Method and Procedure

Preparatory work

Mr A presents this proposal to a steering committee of the area's Chamber of Commerce and discusses with them the membership of the conference and its infrastructure. All potential participants should be individually approached and briefed about the conference. This work can be divided between the members of the Steering Committee. Special attention should be given to the understanding of the working principles of the referent group: the expected results, and what should not be expected from them.

Tentative schedule of a one-evening and two-day search conference

First evening. Getting acquainted with each other and forming the clusters which are the most typical of the area: e.g. employers versus unions, business people versus politicians, farmers versus city-dwellers, bankers versus industrialists, etc. Every member has to choose the cluster in which he or she feels most at home. The cluster is defined on a flipchart. From five to nine clusters are formed. The evening ends with dinner and informal discussion between all the members.

Morning of the first day. Confrontation meeting: each cluster describes itself, its major contribution to the wealth and welfare of the area and a representative of the other clusters describes how it is perceived by him or her and companions. This may be done in an ironic way, making use of the stereotypes current in the area. The purpose of this meeting is to start to work with the difference between the existing anonymous stereotypes and the real people who embody these stereotypes. Ideological enmities are blunted.

Afternoon of the first day. Introduction to the procedures for arriving at an open debate to which every member can contribute. The method permits the visualization of the network of interest groups and of common interests irrespective of the origin of the member. New clusters are formed around the issues relevant for individual members of the conference. (The method referred to is described by Stafford Beer in *The Heart of Enterprise*[15] and in the forthcoming *Team Tensegrity*.)

Two sessions are held. One session is diverging: the number of issues is illimited, the freedom to move from one interest group to another is complete. In the second session an initial converging and filtering is done. For the first time the new clusters start to define themselves: membership of the core of the cluster is definitive. A cluster is able to define a major aspect of the regional development for which they commit themselves to participate in the definition of a joint project.

The clusters report back the results of their work. These are discussed by the other clusters.

Before- and after-dinner informal meetings between members are held for editing the work already done or for taking up *ad hoc* issues which were not dealt with in a cluster.

Morning of the second day. An introduction is given about the minimal elements of a good project definition. Each cluster, whose members share a common issue, applies the principle to the definition of two projects. The definitions of the projects are discussed with the members of the other clusters, so that the quality of the final definition is much enhanced.

Afternoon of the second day. The whole afternoon is devoted to design a communication action plan to the outside world, to make action plans for the next steps in the realization of the projects and of the next meeting of the referent organization.

A final evaluation of the results ends the conference. That was the conclusion of the proposal.

6.6 APPRECIATION, APPRECIATIVE SYSTEMS AND APPRECIATIVE ENQUIRY

To complete the treatment of the value-systems domain and as an introduction to the spiritual one, it is useful to examine the meaning of the term 'appreciation' by Srivastva[3] and Vickers[1]. Both use it to understand and intervene in human affairs. Vickers has been mainly a practitioner and only at the end of his career did he start to conceptualize his experiences in the public and private sectors, where he assumed major responsibilities. Suresh Srivastva is also a reflective practitioner and has consistently tried to bridge the gap between the academic world and that of practice. Both write about their understanding of activities in the value-systems domain. Srivastva has his roots in what is called the Eastern spiritual traditions, Hinduism and Buddhism, while Vickers declared himself to be a 'product of an English classical education' and has thus strong roots in the Western humanities.

Western tradition has always been strong in 'critical' thinking and the critical method of dealing with value systems. A major work by Vickers is called: *The Art of Judgment*. Judgement and criticism are etymologically equivalent: 'judgement' has a Latin origin and 'criticism' a Greek one. Criticisms and judgements have been given in Western intellectual culture the connotation of negative implications. Exactly in the same way, the word 'diagnosis', which etymologically means an assessment of a state of affairs, has received in our tradition the connotation of looking for symptoms of sickness. In Chapter 2 I have broadened the meaning of diagnosis, when I defined systems diagnosis as a means for generating data for the audit information process. Hence the interesting definition of Vickers in his *Freedom in a Rocking Boat*[16]. 'To account for the *appreciated* world—which is, after all, one of the most assured facts of our experience—I postulate that experience, especially *the experience of human communication*, develops in each of us readiness to notice particular aspects of our situation, to *discriminate* them in particular ways and to *measure* them against particular standards of comparison, which have been built up in similar ways.' (Italics are mine.) Valuing is here seen as comparing, measuring against standards. Changing value systems is only possible if these standards are changed.

Srivastva and Cooperrider write in their *Appreciative Inquiry in Organizational Life*: 'Principle 1: Research into the social (innovation) potential of organizational life should begin with appreciation. This basic principle assumes that every social system 'works' to some degree—that it is not in a complete state of entropy—and that a primary task of research is to *discover, describe, and explain* those social innovations, however small, which serve to give 'life' to the system... *the appreciative approach takes its inspiration from the current state of "what is"*.' (Italics are mine.) The value behind this statement reflects what I understand as the Buddhist stance of *compassion*. Whatever is, is worthwhile to be and to develop. Valuing is in this world view much more keeping in touch with what is, maintaining a relation with it and postponing a judgement, which endangers this relation.

But ultimately, Vickers and Srivastva meet each other, because Vickers also sees the outcome of the appreciative process as actions to maintain, modify or elude relevant relationships with the 'lifeworld', the flux of interacting events and ideas. Both express in their own way that, when involved in activities in the value-systems domain, developments are essentially non-teleological. Srivastva refers to the ongoing activity of organizing as a miracle of co-operative human interaction, without the need of an organization as end-state. As Checkland and Casar[2] write succinctly about Vickers' concept of an appreciative system: an appreciative system is a process whose products— cultural manifestations—condition the process itself. It is operationally closed via a structural component (the flux of events and ideas) which ensures that it does not through its own actions reproduce an exact copy of itself.

Working and intervening in the value-systems domain requires permanent attention to the continuity of the process. Goals, strategies, decisions cannot belong to this domain. For this reason, most of the organization and management literature has a poor understanding of activities belonging to this domain. Nevertheless, these activities are the ground upon which decisions, innovations and institutions are developing. When one looks at what are normally perceived as political activities, (I have defined politics as the activities where value systems are debated and developed) we are far from the value-systems domain. Fortunately, in spite of political theories, obsessed by power and decision making as they are, value systems are continuously developing.

REFERENCES

1. Vickers, G. (1983). *The Art of Judgment*, Harper and Row
2. Checkland, P. and Casar, A. (1986). Vickers' concept of an appreciative system: a systemic account, *Journal of Applied Systems Analysis*, 13, University of Lancaster
3. Srivastva, S. and Cooperrider, D. (1987). *Appreciative Inquiry in Organizational Life, Research in Organizational Change and Development*, Vol. 1, JAI Press Inc.
4. Habermas, J. (1988). *On the Logic of the Social Sciences*, Polity Press
5. Maturana, U. and Varela, F. (1987). *The Tree of Knowledge*, Shambhala Publications Inc.
6. Block, P. (1987). *The Empowered Manager*, Jossey-Bass
7. Girard, R. (1977). *Violence and the Sacred*, Johns Hopkins University Press
8. Jaques, E. (1983). *A General Theory of Bureaucracy*, Heinemann
9. Trist, E. (1979). Referent organizations and the development of inter-organizational domains, Lecture to the Academy of Management, 39th Annual Convention, Atlanta
10. Checkland, P. (1981). *Systems Thinking, Systems Practice*, Wiley
11. Pascal, B. (1978). *Pensées*, Seuil
12. Schecter, D. (1991). Beer's 'Organizational Tensegrity' and the challenge of democratic management, *Systems Practice*, 4, No. 4

13. Habermas, J. (1984, Vol. 1, 1987, Vol. 2). *The Theory of Communicative Action*, Boston
14. Ormaechea, J.M. (1991). *The Mondragon Cooperative Experience*, Mondragon Corporacion Cooperativa
15. Beer, S. (1979). *The Heart of Enterprise*, Wiley
16. Vickers, G. (1972). *Freedom in a Rocking Boat*, Penguin Books

Chapter 7

___ Beyond the 20-year Time Span: the Spiritual Domain

I am able to give only an indication of the processes belonging to this recursion level, which starts with process level 7, from 20 years onwards, and goes much further in time. Only a desire to complete the whole conceptual framework stimulates me to write this short chapter.

One characteristic is that the processes in this domain are strongly linked to individuals. Because of the very large work capacity (Jaques defines work capacity as the maximum time perspective people have when actually involved in doing things), these individuals have worked through their own death, by means of the experience of the deaths of others, and this experience becomes the major source of their creativity. The way we human beings deal creatively and consciously with our deaths, how we express it, I call the path to the spiritual (Figure 7.1). It is clear that the processes belonging to this domain are very personal in nature, but, paradoxically, have a universal component.

The conscious working through of two fundamental universal human paradoxes are the fount of activities in the spiritual domain:

• My existence and my self-consciousness, the development of my identity, is due only to my participation in a social context, to my being and becoming with others. What I can conceive as my life as an individual is only possible as I relate to others. Even my egocentricity or egoism is the result of my relations with others, of my altruism, my relatedness. One of the most beautiful expressions in literature of this paradox is Robinson Crusoe, whose survival is only possible through the reconstruction of his original social world, which he keeps as a living memory. In a century when individualism became a value Daniel Defoe described the essence of life as an individual. Even when no-one else is sharing Crusoe's life, he survives as a network of relations. He creates a work system on his island. Man Friday is a logical consequence of his endeavours. The same paradox is expressed in a complementary way by Kenneth Gergen in his *The*

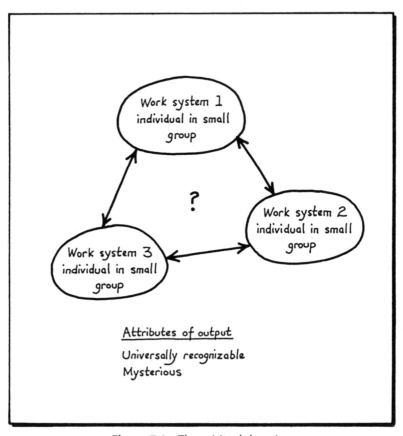

Figure 7.1 The spiritual domain

Saturated Self[1], where he describes the Robinson Crusoe of a world where events and ideas from everywhere are accessible to every individual at every moment through the electronic media. This post-modern Crusoe lives in his island, named Virtual World.

• The most significant experience of that relatedness comes when, in fact, relations are broken. In terms of Heidegger, when self-evidences are breaking down they become part of our consciousness and of our language. And the deaths of those who are near and dear is, for me, the most significant breakdown of a relation. Although I cannot imagine my own death I can experience it as an individual through the deaths of others, the disappearance of all their relationships. Traces of funeral rites and human artefacts have always been linked by palaeontologists to human culture. Human perception of life and death, human creativity and destructivity, production and consumption are the contradictions at the roots of human activity systems, of work systems.

Some people work through these paradoxes by expressing them in universally recognized forms, which I should like to define as works of art: from the Bible to the Parthenon, from the Copernican universe to the space-time of Einstein, from the depth of Giotto's paintings to the wisdom of the Tao, from the *Baghavat-Ghita* to the installations of Joseph Beuys. The major characteristic is that these expressions are somehow understandable by all cultures and by people of all ages. The universal depth of humanity can be directly sensed by everyone who is open to his or her own humanity. But, at the same time, all these works keep their mystery. Persons who develop activities on process level 7 refer to these works as the foundation of their value system. There is a strong link between ethics, the value-systems domain and aesthetics, the domain of spiritual works of art.

Not all that is called art belongs to this domain. Art can belong to each of the previous three domains. When art is seen as an expression of a work system this should be self-evident. But this discussion could lead us too far astray from the mainstream of this book.

The greatest expression of spirituality in human beings occurs when their life and behaviour heavily influence subsequent generations, although they did not leave any direct traces of their creativity. One can think of Buddha, Socrates, Jesus Christ, Lao Tseu, Mahatma Ghandi, Francis of Assisi and others. They lived creatively and their 'disciples' explicitly refer to the life and death of their 'master' as the foundation of their endeavours and values. In all cases, the death of the 'master' has been transmitted as an ultimate creative act.

The paradox lies in the fact that what people working in the spiritual domain are actually doing cannot easily be differentiated from activities which belong to the first process level. I have tried to illustrate this by the answer given by the fourth stonemason in Section 3.2. The difference lies in the fact that what 'spirituals' do and the way in which they do it has a great impact upon those who have had the opportunity of meeting them. Like the works of art I mentioned, they have confronted me with my own mortality and creativity and have enabled me to work through my own life and death. Not every potter is only a potter. Some of them are creating human universals and meeting them creates lasting memories, in which awe and joy, fear and love stay inextricably intertwined. I apologize to the reader for this very personal account of these experiences. But as these activities are also profoundly human they cannot be excluded from this book. 'Spirituals' are not only making work systems better, they are also making people better human beings. The beauty of activities in the spiritual domain is that they are not secret, abstract or high-brow, they are very specific and concrete, so that sometimes they pass unnoticed.

In spite of the personal character of the above paragraph, I should like to describe the activities in the spiritual domain as for the other three domains.

7.1 GENERIC TRANSFORMATION PROCESS

To materialize through works of art or mere behaviour the universal understanding of one's own mortality.

7.2 BASIC STRATEGIC DILEMMA

To struggle with one's own consciousness of death in a creative way. To live with and live beyond the depression of the loneliness associated with working through one's own death by creating universally recognizable expressions of human life and death.

Each of us has had the opportunity for this kind of experience. To illustrate this, I would like to quote two artists who helped me recently to understand the processes to which I am referring.

Joseph Beuys: One accepts death as the methodology for Creation. Because one desires it, because one has the fundamental insight that without the element of death one cannot live consciously. When one is only interested in life, one might as well be a fish...Who is not dying, before he dies, decays when he dies. (Author's translation.)
Jimmy Durham: When I was a child I grieved that we killed any animal that crossed our path and ate its flesh ... all of the other animals had the same voracious cruelty. We had to cringe in fear. Any animal unable to fear would not be successful. You must kill, and fear death. Mammals, then, as a strategy for survival, developed emotions. But we cannot say that the emotion of fear is primary. Love and fear must be simultaneous. Because every animal, even your boyfriend, has a mouth with some sort of teeth, one cannot easily allow an approach.

Perhaps this chapter can shed some light on why the time parameter, which is so helpful in understanding and improving work systems, has been so much neglected in the literature on organizations. If our consciousness of our life and death and the way we work through them is the foundation of human activities, deployed in all domains, and if organizational and institutional continuity is the ultimate formal objective in Western organizational ideology, all references to temporality must generate some uneasiness.

Therefore it is no surprise that competing for time becomes the new managerial slogan. Value systems are also self-regulating, sometimes in an ironical way. Accelerating production processes, working just-in-time, real-time information (which in fact signifies no time at all), accelerating innovations, even rapid cultural changes in organizations and whole societies, as in the former Soviet Union, will inevitably confront us again with temporality and its fundamental constraints. Just as the gardener who flees as fast as he can to Isfahan, because he saw Death in Beirut, is surprised by Death in Isfahan in the evening, so we will meet the time constraint where we have fled to avoid it.

At the end of the twentieth century and at the end of the Newtonian world view, which looks at time as an independent and reversible variable, we will have to review our perception of time and our own temporality. Prigogine[2] started to work with time as an operator for non-linear dissipative structures. Elliott Jaques[3] has had the great merit of differentiating chronological Newtonian time from the individual time perspective of each human being. We owe it to Joseph Beuys to have consciously built into his works of art ongoing physico-chemical processes of change. Art is indeed the human activity where perpetuity is seen as self-evident. In a discussion with a director of an innovative firm which specializes in all kinds of automatic time-keeping devices it came as a shock to him, but also as an eye-opener, when I mentioned that a new perspective on the time dimension will be at the roots of the coming technological and institutional innovations in the next century. Every viable system uses its own time dimension as an operational factor in its development.

Perhaps it will be painful to be confronted again with our time constraints, but as has been shown by so many people in the spiritual domain, this consciousness will lead us to the foundations of all human creativity.

Here also, it could be possible to give some illustrations of how I deal with my confrontation with spiritual art and artists. I could refer to my written comments of a performance of a young Dutch artist, who expressed the tension between the dead letter of an old text and the life she brought to it by her mere presence, or to the inaugural talk I held for a marvellous exhibition in Belgium with the appealing title of 'In Memory of the Future'. But without the corresponding visual context this does not make much sense. I can only refer the interested reader to my first book , *Over Boundaries, a Theory for People at Work*, which will appear in 1994[4]. Each chapter of the book contains the reproduction of a contemporary work of art and a small comment, which links it to the theme of that chapter.

REFERENCES

1. Gergen, K. (1991). *The Saturated Self*, Basic Books
2. Prigogine, I. (1980). *From Being to Becoming*, Freeman
3. Jaques, E. (1982). *Forms of Time*, Heinemann
4. Hoebeke, L. (1994). *Over Boundaries, a Theory for People at Work*, Kunst en Projekten, Zedelgem, Belgium

Chapter 8

_ Starting to Play with the Framework

8.1 PERSONAL REFLECTIONS UPON YOUR OWN WORK AND CONTRIBUTIONS

We have travelled a long way through the whole diversity of human activities and I hope that somehow, through the examples given, the reader has a feeling for assessing which kind of contribution belongs to which kind of generic process. Some of the process levels may seem utterly irrelevant. Do not bother about this. Skip them. It is clear that this framework does not provide an unequivocal way to classify 'objectively' all the activities and contributions of your colleagues and yourself. The purpose of the language is to help the debate between the various actors in common endeavours to help them to position their contributions.

For this reason, the best way to start to work with the framework is to start with your own work reality, which you share with colleagues. Try to define for yourself to which transformation process your major contributions are applied. Try to define who are the clients and the stakeholders of this process. Define for yourself, through the time-span parameter, on which process level this process belongs. And then refer to the generic descriptions defined in the corresponding process level and try to use the conceptual framework to discover the essence of the process.

If the discoveries made are rather surprising, be patient and interchange them with friends and colleagues who, in your opinion, are engaged in the same process.

Many people in head offices, in governmental agencies or even in supranational bodies are working in the added-value domain but are very distant from the place where the real work is done. Productivity, profitability, efficiency belong essentially to the added-value domain, wherever people involved with these issues are working.

In Western democracies, government is one of the major employers. It is clear that not all of the activities performed by public servants and politicians belong to the value-systems domain. If you work in a public agency, there is a great probability that activities which belong to quite different domains are meeting somewhere in your work environment. Try to use the differentiation of the processes and of their outputs to make some sense out of the contradictory demands made upon you.

If you are working in the non-profit sector, in education, in social welfare, even in sport and if you are interested in organizational theories, you have probably been struggling with the bias towards business in the literature. I invite you to try to define the added value of your organizations in terms of the output characteristics, appreciated by your clients or patients. My own experience in non-governmental organizations is that this exercise makes clear sometimes in a painful way that choices between the many service/market/technology combinations cannot be avoided to make your organization successful in terms of customer satisfaction.

Mintzberg[1] has indicated that the issues around centralization and decentralization have an oscillatory behaviour with a cycle of about 10 years. You are possibly involved in such issues. Mostly they are raised in terms of persons or facilities and not of activities.

For many companies the term 'decentralization' refers only to a geographical dimension. Banks, insurance companies or others, which have distributed services are typical examples. When the local agencies receive a profit and loss responsibility as a consequence of decentralization, internecine struggles for certain interesting accounts which have no geographical rationale for their organization become inevitable. It is worth using the output attributes of the added-value domain to try to match them with the formal organizational boundaries and responsibilities to be able to clarify a whole series of organizational problems.

Many large industrial complexes such as petrochemical, or multi-product facilities are trapped in a double bind as soon as headquarters follows the latest fashion of creating business units and outsourcing activities which do not belong to what is called the core business. Technological interdependencies at the facility level are in flagrant contradiction to the product logic behind the business units. Looking at what can be decentralized on process level 1 (the primary process) and what has to be kept centralized on process level 2 (the creation and maintenance of the means) can be a useful exercise to make some sense of the difficulties.

Research and Development divisions are always struggling with centralization–decentralization issues. Here also, the classification of the activities in the added-value and innovation domains can create a language in which these issues can be debated. The development activities which have been defined for each process level can then be used to refine the results. In my experience the overcrowding and overloading of many development divisions are caused by the perception that the developments which belong to the different process levels have in some way to be situated in one organizational unit.

Perhaps you find yourself in an organizational context, which is not uncommon. You are involved in activities in the innovation domain, but the management systems, the information and control systems, the reporting and reward systems belong much more to the added-value domain. Then you are bound to see them as irrelevant hindrances, which demand much energy and time.

You have been assigned as the head of a new department or agency or you have had a foreign assignment to represent your business overseas for the first time. The expectation of headquarters or of your boss is that you follow the company policies and procedures regarding personnel, reports, requests for capital, etc. You try to comply, but do not feel happy about it. Unwittingly, you have been assigned to an innovative activity, where the best organizational form is to work with a project team. You can try to define your project as outlined in the Application section of Chapter 5 of this book. Eventually you can start to use the reporting system creatively as a steering tool for your project. You can negotiate to have your budget as an undifferentiated lump sum, which indicates the maximum to be spent during an unpredictable course of events. But, most importantly, you make efforts to maintain personal contacts with your major stakeholders at headquarters. Lobbying is more important for you than reporting.

You are heading a specialist staff department but as your staff is competent and works independently, you ask yourself what exactly is your role as a manager. Probably you see if you can create with colleagues in other specialist staff departments some joint concept which uses interdisciplinary synergies and try to define a project along these lines. In any case, you have to monitor the relevance of your specialty and have to look outside your own organization for data. Perhaps you want to contribute to a professional association to define standards and rules of conduct. You may develop activities on process levels 5 (whole-system innovations) or 6 (value-systems domain of your professional area).

Perhaps you belong to the group of people who perceive organizational boundaries as hindrances. You are a member of different professional associations to which you devote much time. You like to hear about new developments and, when possible, travel to conferences. Your colleagues complain that you are away more often than is necessary—for instance, giving lectures to students. You enjoy intellectual debate. In fact, if being independent or freelance did not require that you must earn your living in other ways, you would prefer not to belong to an organization.

You are the marketing director of a large consulting firm. One of the tasks you appreciate most is to organize in the lecture theatre of headquarters, which has been built under your persistent requests, conferences and debates for which you invite successful 'strange' characters, travelling the world to develop their latest ideas. You convince your fellow-directors of the value of these events to point out their importance for the corporate image and the fact that the firm is in the front line of relevant developments in the field. But you angrily override a colleague who suggests that perhaps it would be useful to make a cost-benefit analysis of these events. You are working definitely in the value-systems domain. If it has not happened already, you will soon become confronted by your own physical and psychological constraints.

You started your career in a study group sponsored by a trade union or a political party and feel increasingly less at ease with the conservatism and rigidity of the constituencies and its representatives in the 'system'. You are annoyed most by the discrepancy between what is said in slogans and propaganda and what is done. You know that in real life right and wrong cannot be identified with parties or factions. You are looking for a sinecure as a representative on one or other advisory board of an association or organization, which in your opinion is doing useful work without being in the media spotlight. You hope to be able to meet colleagues who belong to adversarial parties or interest groups with whom you can debate and share your views 'far from the madding crowd'. Your main interest is in activities in the value-systems domain.

Once you have tried to reflect upon your own interests and activities and have found the concepts of the previous chapters useful, you can start to make a system diagnosis of a work system, which you like in spite of the fact that you think that it is problem-ridden. You start to answer the following questions in terms of the domain in which you think the system operates.

How do we manage to provide products and services for our customers, which satisfy them more or less, while we see so many things going wrong, so many bureaucratic meaningless procedures, such a lack of motivation, etc.?

How are we still able to introduce innovations while the business units are not interested at all, while funds are drying up, while there is such a resistance to assimilate them?

How are we able to influence the power caucus, with all its prerogatives, its stereotyping, its innate inertia, so that somehow it seems to understand that values are changing, that the work ethic is no longer what it was, that patriotism and other forms of loyalty are disappearing?

Although this kind of system analysis may sometimes generate painful reactions, in general, the discoveries made are enlightening and give us courage to continue the search for relevance and for understanding the complexities of human work and its meaning. Sharing the exercise with colleagues may even produce fun and joy. Once one discovers how the system is achieving its purpose, in contrast to the way it is supposed to work according to current organizational theories, hope is very near. And hope is the fertile ground for life and development.

In order to convey some of this hope I propose that you read in the next section an alternative blueprint of the world of institutions and organizations, which is my way of using the framework creatively. Although at first this blueprint of a networked world of work may look very different from what exists now, it is based upon a system analysis of actual work systems and organizations. It is as much descriptive as prescriptive. I hope that you will at least be stimulated by it and, at best, enjoy it so that you can start to build your own framework with the help of this blueprint.

8.2 A CONTROVERSIAL BLUEPRINT OF THE WORLD OF WORK

In the first section of this chapter I wrote that it is much more relevant to look at the world of work and organizations as if they were networks of work systems, processes and relations, rather than taking for granted the dominant paradigm of monolithic, hierarchical formal organizations and institutions. Now that we have all the elements of the conceptual framework, I can make a map of the network of activities, processes and work systems, which can be discovered by studying the official institutional dogma of free markets, governments, the separation between the economic domain, the political and social domain and the cultural domain. As you may have already noted, the language I have developed does not take these separations for granted. A visualization of the blueprint which I propose can be seen in Figure 8.1.

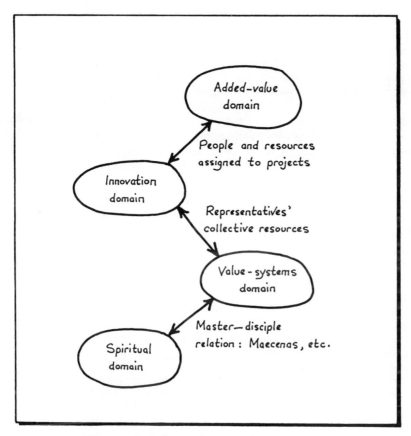

Figure 8.1 Relations between the four domains

Controversy 1: Economics

Disciplinary boundaries are much like organizational boundaries, they are irrelevant for understanding the phenomena which, they claim, belong to their domain. The 'science' which has the most problems in defining its boundaries with a minimum of systemic relevance is 'economics'. It is also the science which claims to be above all value systems, by investigating in a value-free way the valuation processes in human transactions. All human values become 'objectifiable': this means that the reification of processes and relations is at the core of economic science (which is far from economic thinking and practice). To illustrate this, I refer to two classics of economic science.

> The annual labour of every nation is the fund which originally supplies it with all the necessaries and conveniences of life which it annually consumes, and which consists always in the immediate produce of that labour, or in what is purchased with that produce from other nations. Adam Smith, *Introduction to The Wealth of Nations.*[2]
>
> Economics is the study of how men and society *choose*, with or without the use of money, to employ *scarce* resources to produce various commodities over time and distribute them for consumption, now and in the future, among various people and groups in society. Paul Samuelson, *Economics.*[3]

Adam Smith had no problems in making a direct relation between power and economics by defining the 'nation' as the system which he wanted to investigate. The value judgement behind this choice is still current. The GNP, which is only partially meaningful for Western states and nations but completely irrelevant for countries where power still has its origin in quite different rationales, is used as an idol to compare the development between 'nations'. Even worse, Michael Porter[4], who makes useful comments about strategies in the added-value domain, extrapolates these into 'nations', forgetting that competitive nations are nations at war. Even Adam Smith refers in Book III, Chapter IV of *The Wealth of Nations* to the relevant system of governance, which is at the base of sound economic behaviour.[2]

> How the commerce of the towns contributed to the improvement of the country...Thirdly, and lastly, *commerce and manufacturers gradually introduced order and good government*, and with them, the liberty and security of individuals, among the inhabitants of the country, who had *before lived almost in a continual state of war with their neighbours, and of servile dependency upon their superiors.* This, though it has been the least observed, is by far the most important of all their [towns'] effects. Mr Hume is the only writer who, so far as I know, has hitherto taken notice of it [My italics.].

This is to the credit of Adam Smith. I will return to it when I apply the conceptual framework to the value-systems domain and thus to relevant boundaries of political systems. I wish only to mention here that in the history of Western democracies, cities, as democratic islands, have always had an adversarial relation to the 'Prince', who has not been an example of economic behaviour but much more the champion of war and waste. This is still the case for all kinds of institutions and organizations, which use their major value language to say that people 'belong' to them: states in the first place, but also large corporations, supranational agencies, etc. At the end of this century we are becoming aware that 'economic' behaviour and 'power' relations are essentially adversarial in nature. The value system behind the use of aggregates as the unit of investigation and language, instead of networks of work systems, takes for granted the existence of 'absolutist' law and order. Economic laws are used for the legitimation of economic war and its victims.

It was quite a shock for management students in St Petersburg when I made them aware that the actual rulers of Russia and their high priests, Western economic advisors, were using exactly the same language as their previous Communist rulers. 'You have to suffer, to create paradise for the next generations.' In other words, all this waste of material, of human potential, of creativity is a necessary economic law. Alas, what happened to the beautiful word 'economy' in its meaning of parsimony!

And what of CEOs or other board members who receive their compensation and perks in terms of the work relations which they have demolished just as generals receive accolades for the number of casualties they caused? Their legitimation, the inexorable law of ruthless competition, sounds very similar to the language of all kinds of warlord: ethnic cleansing does not belong only to the political realm!

In contradiction to Adam Smith, Paul Samuelson confuses all kinds of aggregation levels in his definition of economics. In one phrase he speaks of 'men', 'society', 'various people' and 'groups in society'. It comes as no surprise that to exemplify his basic view of economics he uses the metaphor of the choice between butter and guns. In practice, the groups and lobbies opting for guns have no problem in also having butter on their daily bread—compare events in Somalia or Bosnia. Metaphors are much more revealing than is sometimes thought: they are expressions of the explicit or implicit values behind 'value-free' utterances.

Even the use of the term 'shock therapy' in the context of economic systems is indicative of the confusing of all kinds of systemic levels. On the individual level, shock therapy is a controversial issue. Only socially damaging individual behaviour may, in rare circumstances, be invoked for applying this kind of therapy. People who use this word in an economic and social context are so arrogant that they define a whole network of socio-economic relations as dangerously crazy. Who needs shock therapy in any case?

After these far from value-free controversial statements, I will try to apply the conceptual framework to what I like to define as the 'economic' domain *par excellence*, the added-value domain.

8.2.1 Relations between Work Systems in the Added-value Domain

As mentioned earlier, the added-value domain is the domain of the work systems which create added value for each other. The relations between work systems in this domain are not conditioned by ideological free-market principles. One seldom finds people in these systems who are only price conscious. The relation between supplier and client is largely price independent, at least when both parties also have a personal relationship. Normal consumers choose their shops, even in the marketplace, because the relation with their supplier, his or her knowledge of their needs and requirements, is part of the product/service provided. Changing buying habits is always a longer-term activity. It belongs at least to process level 2.

One of the reasons I left my bank was its tendency to change its junior staff every three months. The new clerks did not recognize me. In the same way, although prices are lower in a new grocery at the same distance as the one she uses currently, my wife is reluctant to change, because she has to learn her way through the shop's shelves and the methods of payment.

Long-standing customer–supplier relations are much stronger than the obsessional search for the cheapest one as suggested by the free-market principle. These relations are essential in the added-value domain. Sometimes they are formalized through contracts, but often in large organizations they are implicit. To get something done, I know my network of suppliers. When persons are moved too frequently, work systems become inflexible and difficult to manage. *The paradox is that stable social networks are the best guarantee of flexible work-system performance.* Both parties, the supplier and the customer, internal or external, appreciate what they mean for each other, they understand the real added value. This is one of the major lessons which can be drawn from Japanese management principles.

The above statement in italic is essential in understanding the term 'organizational flexibility'. When organizations are seen as power systems flexibility expresses itself easily in the power to move people around. That may be done by a production supervisor on the shopfloor, who every day, in terms of the availability of those present and the requirements of the job, assigns 'his staff' to different tasks and places. It may also be carried on by 'management developers', who wish to assess the flexibility of 'high potentials'. There is a direct correlation between this kind of flexibility and the number of bureaucratic procedures and the inertia shown by the system itself.

A utilities company had a policy that staff who were to make their career in head office should be assigned as power-plant managers for two years. This enabled the employee instructed to restructure the organization of the plant to show managerial potentiality. A thorough study of the way workers were performing maintenance activities showed that this had continued unchanged since the start-up of the power plant. Electrical and mechanical maintenance each had its own instruction manual. Fortunately, the mechanical and electrical engineers formed long-lasting teams, who had their disputes but who also knew how to keep the system in running order.

Because of the preponderance of customer–supplier relations, the added-value domain belongs to the area of 'economic' and 'market' transactions. But these transactions are never anonymous, they are embedded in a social network of known people.

The automation of a sale of farm products was a complete failure because it permitted farmers to offer their products from computer terminals on their farms. The physical presence of themselves and their colleagues in the auction hall was essential for making the 'market'.

Even abstract 'as if' monetary transactions in dealing rooms can never take place without a known network of people. The failure of the 'Big Bang' in the London Exchange Market was due to the very naive ideological market image created by Margaret Thatcher and her advisers. Although it is worth investigating the added value of all kinds of intermediaries, eliminating them because they seem superficially to inhibit the free flow of goods and services is a means of overruling simple systemic ways of working.

The added-value domain is, in this sense, the marketplace. It is subject not to anonymous laws of supply and demand but to the knowledge that the various partners in the marketplace have of the added value they signify for each other. Markets are not aggregates but networks. And again, markets are to be discovered inside organizations as well as between them. Formal organizational definitions do not help us to detect them. Output specifications and requirements are the material to look for. In large organizations I introduced the concept of formal management contracts between the various work systems in the added-value domain. These contracts use the language of inputs, transformation processes, outputs, specifications and requirements, etc. Using the same language enabled my clients, large 'kombinats' in the former Communist bloc, to restructure themselves following the outlines of the work systems in the added-value domain. Many so-called headquarters activities and services also belong to this domain. An 'open market' for these services was an essential part of improving their performance.

Controversy 2 : Competition

When one looks at the added-value domain as one where customer–supplier transactions take place and when these transactions have also a human relation component, it is worth investigating the meaning of competition in the ideological economic discourse.

Free markets are much more collaborative than competitive and, exactly for that reason, more economic. Competition is the game played within the constraints of collaborative relationships.

During my professional life I have met many organizations operating in the 'free' market. All, with one exception, knew very well who their competitors were and had implicit market and price deals with them. The one who did not failed together with most of its competitors because of the tug-of-war which existed in that sector. But also within organizations, collaboration is a much more economic way of dealing with each other than is competition. Most of the economic transactions between supplier and customer take place inside organizations, or are formally organized between them. Long-term procurement contracts (from 1 to 3 years is quite normal in inter-industrial customer–supplier relations) and co-manufacturing relations lead to much more efficient joint operations. EDI (Electronic Data Interchange) and the concepts of lean production and management in fact reduce the number of possible suppliers and require from each of the partners stringent rules of the game (such as just-in-time deliveries), which preclude a quick adaptation to market prices.

The current economic discourse as if competition is the basic mechanism for efficient market relations leads to the incongruency that collaborative relations between the various inter- and intra-organizational work systems are called a competitive weapon.

In fact, the collaborative market is, at the same time, free and efficient. When free choice is available to build long-lasting relationships between customers and suppliers, learning can take place. The normal human tendency to avoid waste, the natural laziness of human beings, who wish to use the least effort to achieve something, always leads learning to a greater efficiency. Economic efficiency is very similar to ecological efficiency: the various species and individuals in the system collaborate and compete with, as its consequence, the viability of the system itself. Self-regulation and, in terms of Maturana and Varela[5], autopoiesis are at the roots of this efficiency.

Only when a value system which bases its ordering upon the concept of an external regulator influences and intervenes directly in the added-value domain do inefficiency and viability problems inevitably occur. For this reason, it is strange to hear governments speak of economic competition and even to have national and supranational agencies who have the task of 'controlling' the freedom of the markets in order to safeguard competition. There is a Flemish saying that when the fox is preaching repentence, farmer, look out for your geese.

When governments use tax or export incentives or directly use the taxpayer's money to 'help' business, they are biasing sound economic behaviour. All great economic dinosaurs have been created by power systems and not out of economic rationality. I can point to the weapons industry in the USA, with its diseconomies throughout the world, or to the intensive agrobusiness in Third World countries, who are exporting food which their hungry population needs. Piore and Sabel[6] stated that big business and economy of scale has superseded successful small and medium-sized enterprises only through active state intervention. Adam Smith could not have imagined that the Wealth of Nations in the twentieth century is created on behalf of the wealth of their populations. The economic 'reforms' in the previously communist bloc countries are creating underdeveloped countries very quickly.

One of the most regulated markets is the labour market: individuals have no free choice if they want to work in return for a decent income. Unemployment makes second-rate citizens. While, in fact, the only wealth-creating factor is human creativity, work is forbidden for a great proportion of the world population in the name of international economic competitiveness. In free-market terms, the black labour market should be stimulated as much as possible to improve the efficient use of 'human capital'. Charles Handy, in his The Future of Work, [7] has made meaningful statements on this perspective on work.

Hence the basic self-regulating mechanism which makes a free market economically efficient is based much more upon freely chosen collaborative relations than upon an imposed competition.

This is one of the surprises once the added-value domain is perceived as a network of work systems, and formal organizational boundaries are taken for what they are: social constructions, with their origins in a feudal map, where boundaries are impenetrable and are indicated by an abrupt change of colour. This model can only generate war and lead to the loneliness and the ultimate death of the fittest, separated from their ecosystem.

Controversy 3: Ownership

The framework which I have developed can, in a controversial way, assume a very specific customer–supplier relation: the ownership relation. Formal and legal boundaries are much more a hindrance than a help in understanding this relation. The confusing of power issues with economic issues makes much debate irrelevant. Mintzberg[8], in his *Power in and around Organizations,* has drawn a horseshoe in which we find sequentially all possible candidates for exerting power upon organizations. Because Mintzberg is still working with accepted formal organizational boundaries, he omitted the most important 'owner' of work systems in the added-value domain. By 'owner' I mean the individual, group or work system which is entitled to stop its activities.

> *The most important owners of work systems in the added-value domain are their clients. Then follow the actors. When the formal owners, the shareholders, are not actors in the work system, they are the least important stakeholders and do not deserve the name 'owner'.*

This is again a direct consequence of the understanding of work systems as the interaction between a system of activities and one of relations between the people involved in it. Ownership in this perspective is a specific kind of relation with the work system. The persons who most appreciate the output of the system, and thus have the greatest incentive to keep the system working or to stop it when it no longer delivers a satisfactory output, are its clients. In practice, they are also the only ones who directly and (sometimes indirectly) pay all the other stakeholders. When the market is really free, the clients of a work system are the most powerful stakeholders.

Processes between raw materials and end-users are now becoming more complex and longer. Many work systems are involved in it, which relate to each other as customer–suppliers. When in practice I take up a client's perspective, while intervening in the added-value domain I restrict my analysis to the direct client of a work system and eventually to the clients of the work system, in which he or she has the role of actor. In an ecology of work systems working in a more or less efficient way one has to trust that the same focus upon the client is taking place throughout the chain of processes and work systems.

The stakeholders who, after the customers, have the greatest interest in the survival of the work system are its actors. If the work is not owned by them, if they have no say in the way they want to satisfy their client, no quality of product or service can be obtained and the work system is at stake. One of the qualities of good managers at any level is precisely their capability to give their colleagues a sense of ownership of the work system to which they contribute. The conceptual framework which I have developed claims that, in practice, the actors in a work system have an ownership relation with it. If not, its viability is in jeopardy. Again, Japanese management practices, which encourage the ownership of the technology and the way of working by its end-users, show the economic soundness of this principle.

A final word has to be devoted to the shareholders. Where they have a real owner relationship with the work systems they formally own, they are fully aware of the priority to be given to the previous stakeholders. In most cases they assume at the same time the role of owner and of actor. Viability is then guaranteed. Institutional ownership or shareholding through the stock exchange is quite another story. In fact, these owners have only a very tenuous relation with the work system itself. Companies and shares are bought and sold, regardless of their real added value. These owners own paper, not companies. When, through mergers or sell-outs, a company had changed owners three times over, say, a period of 2 years, management learned how tenuous this kind of ownership is. Each new owner required new audits and forced a new set of rules on the company. The management saw these rituals as inevitable but completely futile.

The dissociation between economic and financial transactions on the stock exchange will become stronger. Wall Street crashes will become random events, which will have impact only on the gamblers, at least when the managers of the work systems have become aware of the rules of the game and have stopped bothering about the casino business.

Again, economic self-regulation will defeat idealist ownership issues. The fact that the volume of daily financial transactions is made up of 5% of economical transactions and 95% of pure speculation will create the conditions in which the financial world will start to form a highly symbolic transaction platform and hence no longer hinder economic activities. Its impact will diminish under the sound self-regulating abilities of free markets in the added-value domain. The growing importance of barter transactions or of pure accounts receivable–accounts payable entries between customer and supplier is an indication of this ability.

The next bastion to fall under this self-regulating power will be that of international financial transactions and even the tax systems of governments, which are still behaving as if finance is economics. With the downfall of the Communist bloc, power systems all over the world will have an adversarial relation with real economic behaviour. This will be the end of the collusion between economists and national or supranational governments.

8.2.2 Relations between Work Systems in the Added-value and Innovation Domains

Here we have two kinds of relation. The first is a regular exchange of people working on processes on process level 3 (adapting and improving product, services and technologies) with those working on process level 4 (creating new products, services and technologies for a system of known stakeholders). This exchange greatly enhances the transferability and the systemicity of the innovations. At the same time, the added-value domain keeps in touch with what succeeds in the innovation domain.

Many companies have a policy of assigning newly graduated employees to research before they take up operational and/or managerial activities. This creates a difficulty for the company and for the young graduate. An academic career is not focused upon innovation but mostly upon the conservation of bodies of knowledge. A risk-avoiding attitude, which expresses itself in the specific academic 'critical' stance and explains why new things will not work, is perceived as a hindrance for innovators, who have essentially a risk-taking attitude. Innovators then have the tendency to assign research of little practical relevance to the newcomer. His or her estrangement from real innovative work becomes greater. In contrast, the 'critical' stance can be very usefully confronted by operational work, where things are working in any case. Reality quickly replaces 'intellectual criticism' for those who still have the potential to become innovators. The strength of the young graduate, who is permitted to ask questions based upon his or her scientific background, is an asset for operational activities. Young graduates are ideally equipped for making problem or/and systems analysis in the added-value domain.

The second relation between the added-value and innovation domains lies in the fact that the costs incurred in the innovation domain have to be paid for by money generated in the added-value one. This is a strong incentive for managing the basic strategic dilemma between attachment and detachment on level 4. Otherwise, the detachment pull from level 5 has no countervailing power in level 3.

If business units have no say in the way the money is spent in central R&D activities it is likely that riding hobby-horses will creep into R&D. But business units cannot completely determine the R&D budgets, otherwise the risk of innovation will continue to be avoided. Balance and tension have to be maintained. Business units are operating in the added-value domain (levels 1, 2 and 3), good R&D is operating in the innovation domain (levels 3, 4, and 5).

The contract form prevailing between the two domains is through projects. Here the onus of showing their desirability and their feasibility to the work systems in the added-value domain lies within process levels 5 and 4. If one starts to look at the relations between government, universities, research institutes and business from this perspective, many political mechanisms between them are clarified. Again, in practice, the necessary lobbying for funds is far from anonymous. The problem is that the definition and choice of projects has become institutionally non-transparent, because so many institutional intermediaries are involved, that it is surprising that some innovation still succeeds.

It is very rare, in my experience, that project champions have the opportunity of defending the characteristics of their projects themselves. Two processes are running almost parallel and only infrequently meet each other. The first is dominated by red tape in which feasibility studies, 'as if' time schedules, 'as if' cost-benefit analysis are passed from one office to another. As innovations on process level 5 are essentially multidisciplinary in nature and change the rules of the game, they have to pass through the bureaucratic filters of many reviews before they can be funded. The second process is completely different. Experienced innovators have learned that the decision for funding innovations can never take place anonymously. Although they pay lip-service to the bureaucratic paper mill, they put much more effort into meeting the right people, to influencing the power caucus and to debating the value of their endeavours with the different stakeholders.

This way of working through two processes is fundamentally very sound. Innovations should not be welcomed but should be seriously tested on their attributes: desirability, feasibility, transferability and systemicity. But this double process could be made much more efficient if it was managed as one dialectical process between conservation and innovation by the same group of persons. The reason this happens so seldom is that in the value system of progressive modernism, innovations have to be seen as intrinsically good. This leads me to the next controversial statement.

Controversy 4: There is never a need for innovations

The myth that everyone has to be a champion of innovation is dispelled very quickly when one looks at how the system really behaves. Machiavelli was a much keener observer than the innovation ideologists. Too many cooks in the added-value domain, from government, business, academia, etc., spoil the broth. The language I propose here may help to make project definition and project choice more transparent, hence more effective and efficient.

One of the major errors of that myth is to state that innovations must be marketable: this is a contradiction in terms, once the revolutionary characteristics of real innovations are understood. The only attitude possible is of sharing the risk between the partners involved in them and paying for them. Part of this trust may reside in the fact that the parties feel able to stop an innovation effort if, during the course of its development, its incongruencies become too evident.

Innovations are not needed, they are always the fruit of a want, of an enthusiasm on the part of the innovators. At the basis of any innovation is the vision of an innovator. Perhaps it is for this reason that economists have so much trouble in coming to terms with innovation. Economics belongs to the added-value domain and must be conservative by nature. Innovations are creating new economic ecologies. Metaphorically, a new species is invading the existing ecosystem and changing the prevailing rules of the game. A healthy ecosystem is bound to resist this intrusion. This resistance creates the possibility for newcomers to insinuate themselves into the system. It is a guarantee of transferability and systemicity.

The most difficult innovations are the institutional or organizational ones. This is quite understandable. Technological innovations have a direct impact upon the system of activities and only an indirect one upon the system of relations. Sometimes this appears after the point of no return has been passed. The assimilation expresses itself in the work system by a tacit tolerance. Institutional innovations aim directly at a change in the system of relations in a work system. This is much more threatening to the different stakeholders. Resistance to institutional change is a very healthy immune reaction. It creates organizational fever. In practice reorganization of any kind should only be used as an intervention method, when other ways of keeping the system healthy have failed. By reorganization I mean the reshuffling of relations between the people involved in the system.

As project teams working in the innovation domain are temporary by nature, it is worth creating a base for their members. The reason many projects are continuing and are not transferred to the added-value domain is that the project team members, who have in any case to struggle with the process of ending the project and handing it over to others, have no future after the project. They have the feeling that they have to rebuild completely their network of relations. It could be worth using the relations between industry and university to take care of this need.

At the same time, I am prescribing the relations between the domains and describing them: successful and failed innovations can be analysed in terms of the quality of the relations described. Not only R&D agencies or departments but also the many failed revolutions, which were unable to transform the institutions of the discarded regime, can be looked at in this way. In many cases the anxiety about the point of no return, typical of level 5, has tempted innovators to flee into the future in panic. They then lost their anchoring opportunities.

8.2.3 Relations between the Work Systems in the Innovation Domain

Here the only possible relations are through the exchange of persons in the various project groups and through meetings of people working in them to exchange ideas, concerns and hopes. The exchange of people between projects must take into account the right time frame. If it happens too often, contributions will suffer.

In some project organizations, i.e. those which have project work as their major structuring rationale, I have often found a tendency to create professional project managers. These 'receive' projects to manage and are switched from one project to another. This is a good way of avoiding innovation. The innovation process is looked upon as a normal production process, which can be managed with routine skills and procedures. An innovation is always someone's child: parenthood is not an assignment but a choice.

But there is a tendency for innovative people to stay with the successes of the past, to continue on the same theme. The result is overspecialization or the creation of a style, a school of thought, a dogmatic environment. A major example of this behaviour is found at universities, who are thus losing their potential innovative power. Our segmentation of science and knowledge into disciplines is in direct contradiction to the criteria of systemicity and transferability of innovations. Even academic teaching and the inevitable examinations are much more focused upon the perpetuation of knowledge than the creation of a forum for debates, as sometimes happened in universities in the late Middle Ages.

Some time ago I was invited to give a talk to a student's association about one of the latest management fads: the Learning Organization. When I asked the organizers if they thought that a university was a learning organization, they stated, without any doubt, that it was not. When I asked those members of the audience who were working on PhD theses to ask their neighbours how many would read these theses, uneasy laughter broke out.

Conditions have to be created to maintain an intellectual mobility. Interdisciplinary teams are excellent places to nurture this mobility. Douglas B. Lenat[9], in his studies on heuristics, showed that the most productive inventive heuristics are still analogies and metaphors. This means the application of rules from a given domain to a completely different domain. They are more fruitful than specializations, applying certain rules to a smaller field or generalizations, applying some rules to a broader field.

The best but most incongruous example of an analogical heuristic which I have found was the design of the closing mechanism of a coke-oven door by an analogy with that of a horse's anus. A biologist suggested the analogy to metallurgists and mechanical engineers who had been struggling with the problem for a long time.

At the same time, interdisciplinary project teams and meetings form a good preparatory ground for activities on process level 6.

Controversy 5: Planning versus innovation

What is normally understood as planning is incompatible with the concept of innovation. Innovation activities are indeed inherently uncertain and the development of an innovative idea is full of pleasant and unpleasant surprises. Planning normally means dividing a system of activities into definable subactivities and relating these subactivities to each other by means of a time axis. Now innovative activities, which in fact create their maps and paths during the exploration of an unknown territory, are missing the relevant criteria for division, and stages or key events are unpredictable in time. Nevertheless, the literature on project management is full of planning tools. Perhaps it may be useful in terms of the framework to find the origin of the fascination for combining planning methods and innovation projects.

I was very interested to read how Dupont has continually tried to replicate the process of the invention of polymerization, which led to synthetic fibres, by Carothers in its R&D division without success. No conditions, no planning and decision procedures could guarantee similar discoveries.

It is clear that, as normal human beings, innovators try to cope in a particular way with the uncertainties which they know they have to face. And a very human way to cope with uncertainty is to create an anticipative model of causes and effects of what we intend to do. Certainly, planning can fulfil that function. Things go awry when the language used for this model is inherently flawed by a non-relevant understanding of cause and effect.

Positivistic science, which is still the most current ideology behind innovative efforts, has inherited the confusion of the Greek philosophers between causality as a logical and a chronological construct. If...then still has the two meanings in the positivistic language. It is clear that if innovative activities imply a learning process, it must be full of feedback cycles, where the output of one experience is used as the input of the next set aiming at the same results. Chronologically, the terms 'input' and 'output' lose their meaning, while logically they can be part of meaningful maps for the various parties involved in innovative activities.

I discovered this by the extensive use of PERT planning methods. In these a project result is divided into subactivities which are logically related to one another. Some subactivities can be started logically independently from each other, while others are logically related: logically, a train can move only when there is a railway infrastructure available. But PERT planning also requires putting dates and times on the logical map. This generated a pseudo-certainty regarding time but, in practice, it required many updatings of the map after the events. Planning after the events seemed rather futile to me. Useful logic and useless chronology were confused in one model.

Hence, planning in innovative projects now means for me the joint elaboration by the actors in a project of the logic of the activities, which can be used to debate the status of complex systems of interrelated activities with an uncertain outcome and with unpredictable mutual feedback loops and non-linear mutual causalities.

Project teams involved in multidisciplinary technological innovations draw a map of their contributions to the end-result of the project and their logical interrelations. In this way, persons as well as activities are on the map. When, for example, in a chemico-optical process unsolved problems remain concerning the output range of a chemical process, the 'chemist' can point out the logical consequences of the problems so that the expert in optics, who is ready with his or her contribution, can take over part of the problem by refining the controls of the optical system which he or she designed.

The use of personalized planning which omits time in project work makes things much simpler because it does not aim at predicting an unpredictable future and at creating pseudo-certainty. The latter makes planning very complex and it is used as a justification for explaining why things did not perform as planned (Figure 8.2).

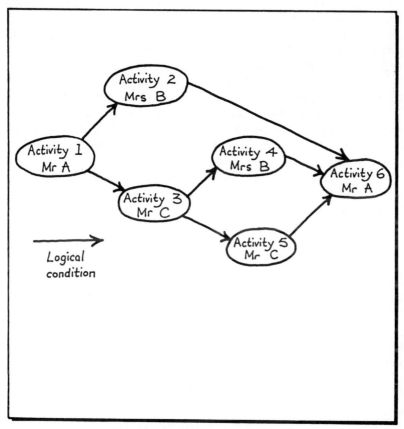

Figure 8.2 Activity planning chart

An instrumentation expert who collaborated in the CERN particle ring-accelerator project in Geneva (a success story in project management circles) told me that the major planning tool for the thousands of contributions, mainly by external suppliers, was the accepted priority to keep to the dates for the installation of the magnets in the ring. These were so internalized as planning priorities by the key actors in the project that without elaborate planning schemes in a self-regulated way all activities were related to this key event. He had the freedom to explore new instrumentation alternatives and to refine his designs and implementations up to a certain point in time. After that point, even if improvements could have been made very quickly, the installation was judged to be acceptable.

8.2.4 Relations between Work Systems in the Innovation and Value-Systems Domains and those in the Value-Systems Domain

Referent groups consist of representatives of various areas which can be influenced by developing value systems. Because, in the innovation domain, the concept of stakeholder is already widespread and because different stakeholders who belong to sometimes contradictory value systems are tolerated, representatives for participating in referent groups are naturally those of the respective stakeholders.

There is a self-regulating selection mechanism at work in the selection of members of referent groups. In my experience, the ability to have strong interpersonal debates about one's own values, without a need to see the results of the debate transformed into decisions, rules, regulations and laws, is uncommon. As we are talking about time spans of 50 years, patience is essential. During the debates the persons present will change their perspectives, their world views, which are strongly interwoven with who they are. Ensuing personal development is an indicator of the relevance of the work of the referent groups.

As the chairman of the board of a non-governmental development aid agency, I had great difficulty in transforming its General Assembly into a referent group. Even though many of the members of the old assembly knew that their decision-making power was almost non-existent and their power to influence was the only reason they agreed to become members, it was some time before they agreed with this perspective.

In referent groups involved in regional development 'planning' one usually finds a non-politician chairing the group. Indeed, elections induce politicians to claim early ownership of 'initiatives', whereas in fact the referent group creates only a strategic language, depending on which different stakeholders take initiatives in their own areas of interest. The major skill of a chairman of a referent group is to permit developments to continue without foreclosing on interesting options too quickly. Strategy in the value-systems domain is about options, not directions.

This means that the relation between the innovation and the value-systems domains occurs only through exchange of persons. Each person should spend at least 5 years in a referent group and then be evaluated by himself and his peers to see if it is worth continuing to participate. In terms of the shifting fields of interest in the innovation domain, new representatives can enter.

I know that these referent groups are actually formalized only rarely. I strongly suggest disclosing them and making their membership known to those people who will be influenced by the results of their work. The debates should not be public but their results should be communicated. The result of the debates will become clear in the innovation domain, or eventually in the spiritual domain of those persons who have their interest in this domain.

Controversy 6: Making the news

We have seen that the output of the value-systems domain is new perspectives upon the stream of ideas and events. From the appreciative systems of the various stakeholders in the debate held in that domain, a new understanding develops and leads to a new way of talking about shared experiences. Originally, daily newspapers were one of the important media to generate debate within the elite clubs of readers. Public opinion was paramount and determined what was worth debating: it was clear by whom certain events and ideas were highlighted. News makers were aware that they were providing elements for debates in the value-systems domain. As it was also readers who paid for their newspapers and journals, the feedback to the news makers was obvious.

Three factors in the added-value domain completely changed the nature of this process:

- The number of readers has grown considerably as a result of the movement towards literacy, which started during the nineteenth century and bore fruit at the beginning of the twentieth. Daily newspapers and the news became personalized commodities. For example, the Viennese cafés, which today still offer daily newspapers to their clients, have lost their debating character, which was still very important before the First World War. The vivid descriptions of them by Hitler in the autobiographical part of *Mein Kampf* are a testimony to this.
- The major clients, i.e. those who are paying for the publication of the daily newspapers, are no longer the readers but the advertisers. Opinions are softened not to offend readers so that more copies are sold, which leads to more advertising and more income. News has also become a commodity. It is given the same task as advertisements: to attract the attention of potential consumers.
- The electronic media have become substitutes for this commodity. These have never had a tradition of stimulating debate. Their unidirectional 'broadcasting' character places them in the area of what I call propaganda. From the beginning, they have been opinion makers, either because they were in the hands of governments, who used them as a means of control, or they belonged to businesses of the advertisement sector, also dedicated to propaganda.

Moreover, news makers as propagandists have taken over the fallacy of positivistic science: they perceive themselves as value-free objective observers of human affairs. In the value domain they do not perceive themselves as stakeholders in the debates between the various 'appreciative' systems. It is worth noticing the power relations between journalists and the 'powerful'. When presidential or other candidates debate in front of the cameras, journalists take the role of moderators, the most powerful position. At press conferences they assume the part of judges of the truths or falsehoods spoken by those whom they interview. This leads to a parasitic love–hate relation between the two major propaganda makers in our societies: politicians and journalists.

In this way the personalized character of real debates in the value-systems domain is lost and is replaced by the artificial reality of the anonymous public opinion debates eventually legitimated by so-called scientific opinion polls. This has two consequences relative to the activities in the value-systems domain:

- One of the major elements of this propaganda is that values are eroding: this is stated by politicians and news makers alike. In fact their perception is coherent with the way in which these propagandists avoid any kind of real feedback, necessary in the development of 'appreciative' systems.
- Second, as human beings cannot avoid developing activities in the value-systems domain, the creation of new appreciative systems happens outside the sphere, where originally they had an institutional place: the political realm and the realm of the news makers. Touraine[10] has written of the difficulty in identifying the proponents of contemporary social movements with classical sociological groups and Galbraith[11] has described the debasement of the public democratic political discourse.

Therefore, in conclusion, I make two controversial statements:

- Either the credibility of politicians and news makers will erode further, because they have become unaware of the basic mechanisms by which values are created and other political realms are in the making. 'Black' politics and 'black' news will proliferate in the same way that 'black' economies are gaining importance. The political and news makers of the future are in the making outside their normal institutional context.
- The political and news-maker institutions will become aware of their fundamental propagandistic nature and find new ways of restoring the personalized feedback systems which are essential for relevant debates in the value-systems domain. A completely new way to use the electronic

media is required. One of the causes of the problem is also its remedy. Sophisticated communication technologies can bring together those persons who have contributions to make in the value-systems domain so that real debates can take place. Stafford Beer, in his *Platform for Change*,[12] has made interesting experiments on how to measure the 'eudaimonic' state of social systems. By eudaimonic, he means a general status of good or bad feelings about the current state of affairs without the necessity of analysing the origins of these feelings. An aggregate eudaimonic indicator could then interactively be used when certain issues are covered by the media and by politicians.

I think that the above explains why, when I am working with referent groups, I avoid the presence of the media during the debates unless their protagonists agree to take on the role of fully fledged stakeholder representatives, instead of objective observers. At the same time, the results of the work in the referent group are carefully communicated to the media, taking into account the propagandistic nature of their communication. This rule is also applied by all referent groups who have had some success. This has nothing to do with secrecy and 'elitist', anti-democratic traits: it is the only way to defend a development search process from being stopped too early by primitive propagandistic statements on right or wrong.

I do not wish to take sides in the recurrent conflict between media and politicians. As both parties still belong to and are maintained by living work systems, their relation forms an essential contribution to the ecology of politics, hence of work systems in the value-systems domain. My major concern is to improve work systems. One way of doing this is to point to the systems of activities and relations to which the two parties are contributing. Propaganda is normal and healthy human behaviour: it feeds the stream of events and ideas, which are essential to developing value systems. What I am criticizing are common ideological stances of both parties as if they do not belong to the realm of living, fallible and vulnerable work systems, as if they could take a position above the 'madding crowd', while in fact they are at its core. Improvement in their functioning will come through the personalization of their relationship, through the generative, tolerant, dialectical and congruent nature of their activities and their relations. There is nothing wrong with power relations as long as they are declared as such and are made transparent to their beneficiaries and victims. In this way I arrive at the seventh controversy.

Controversy 7: The scale of representative democracies

The most adequate metaphor with which I can describe my vision of a democratic world from the perspective of the framework I have developed is an ecological system of a great diversity of value systems. The non-teleological development of this ecosystem implies minimal conditions: although values may disappear and new ones may enter the system, as a species in a biological ecosystem, self-regulating mechanisms have to be maintained so that the system as a whole can survive, adapt and develop. Value diversity is as essential as biodiversity. This in itself is a value statement. For this reason, I have stressed the qualities of activities in the value-systems domain: generativeness, tolerance, dialectics and congruence. These qualities seem to be the minimal requirements for maintaining a value diversity in the system. And for this reason, I refer to democracies in this section.

However, Western democracies have been confronted by a paradox from the beginning. The principles of modern Western democracies have their roots in a reinterpretation of the democratic principles in the ancient Greek city-states and the form they started to take in the city-states of the late Middle Ages. The founding fathers of the modern democracies tried to graft these principles onto their heritage from the absolutist nation-states of the eighteenth century. These were remnants of the feudal territorial subdivisions between warlords against which precisely the city-states fought to maintain their 'democratic liberties'. Two conflicting political structures, the free city-states and the feudal kingdoms, were merged. One of the most delicate operations with which engineers are confronted is the upgrading of prototypes. We have seen that, in systemic terms, when the number of relations is growing, at a certain moment newly emergent characteristics become preponderant and instead of a 'larger' system, we are confronted with a 'new' one. This is exactly what happened with modern Western democracies. The absolutist non-democratic character of nation-states was merged with the democratic character of the city-states.

By 'absolutist' I mean the integration of all realms of human affairs into one overarching structure. As a citizen I still belong to my nation-state as serfs belonged to their feudal lord: I am obliged to fight its wars and to give it part of the fruits of my work through taxes. In exchange, it provides me with a certain amount of protection against human and natural enemies and hence a sense of security. Even in strongly decentralized states we still see today that defence, foreign affairs, home affairs, justice and the treasury belong to the federal government. They are the relics of the feudal, territorial perspective.

Through technological developments this principle of territoriality came under pressure. Communications, travel and economic transactions have created a more open world. At the same time, the realm of human affairs has greatly increased in complexity and diversity. Perhaps we have the same freedom as a century ago, but now we are confronted with many more alternatives and choices. Subsequently, the feudal integrative remnants of Western democracies have reacted by multiplying the number of government domains: from health care to the building of infrastructures, from the running of state-owned enterprises to the payment of state-owned artists as in the Netherlands. All these domains are seen as separate realms and the complexity has been managed through the feudal reflex of creating new territories: culture, social welfare, health care, education, science and technology, transport, post and telecommunications, etc. Once again, more of the same has led to a new emerging system.

Devolution of integrative power to regions is on the agenda of most Western democratic governments. In some cases this leads through old nationalistic territorial reflexes to new nation-states. In a self-regulating way the scale of democracies is again downsized to its original dimension: a city-state or a region. In fact, this is the dimension in which representative democracies can work: the debates in the value-systems domain can avoid being trapped in ideological sterile propaganda only when the inter-personal relations between the various stakeholders are expressed in tangible results in the innovation or added-value domains. Social, economic, political and cultural development can be dealt with in a systemic way only if it is embedded in a shared material and biological realm. Ideas are sterile unless they materialize. Integrative democratic governments are essentially small-scale governments: the size of a Swiss canton, or of a city like Glasgow.

My experience with regional development in a democratic context puts a serious question mark against general elections as a means of appointing representatives in governmental bodies. In fact, in regions the various representatives of different stakeholders form lobbying groups which have a strong influence upon the 'elected' politicians. Decisions and choices in democratic systems are not made by so-called 'legislative' bodies, but by strong and healthy lobbying groups: employers, trade unions, party members, bankers, farmers, etc. The 'parliament' has the role only of legitimating the 'binding advice' arising within the lobbies. In fact, the quality of these lobbies is what determines the quality of governments. This is no surprise when it is considered from the perspective of activities in the value-systems domain. Democracies could become much more transparent and in this way gain a much greater credibility if these mechanisms could be made overt. This can easily be done in regions, because in fact, the persons interested in the body politic know the strength of lobbying groups and who are the influential people to talk to when they wish to influence decisions. Elections are essentially non-systemic, because they are based upon mathematical aggregations of votes, without any insight into the relational nature of the work in the value-systems domain. Since antiquity, head counting in whatever context has been an absolutist way of legitimation. Emperors and kings always have used censuses to boast about their personal power.

When the democratic systems are larger, elections as a way of choosing representatives really pervert the basic concept of democracy. It is as if, between the individual and the representative, there is no place for any work system in any domain. All relations are bypassed in terms of an aggregation rationale. An ecosystem is reduced to the sum of the samples of the different species, without any concern for the ecosystemic relations between them. Human systems become equivalent to 'gases' where each molecule is 'independent'. The fallacy of economic theory is transferred to the fallacy of political practice. Aggregates are non-governable and non-manageable: they reduce to a licence for irresponsible behaviour. Fortunately, in Western democracies, even elected people belong to systems to whom they are responsible. As long as these systems are sufficiently transparent to the various actors, democracy works.

Controversy 8: Global through local

The psychological and physiological constraints of the span of relations which governs all human activity are both a blessing and a curse. A blessing, because they limit our impact upon events and ideas and refute our ambition of global thinking and global acting. Necessarily we have to leave the delusion of creating or controlling 'our global world'. Eventually we can use the various discourses about this world when we influence our small network of relations, but we are never in full control of the consequences of what we do say and do or neglect to say or do. This is a fact as hard for a gardener in the White House, who can work but cannot determine the results of his gardening, as for the President of the United States, who can talk but has no control upon what is done with his words. No species is in control of the ecology of value systems. This guarantees the survival and the development of the ecosystem.

They are a curse because, through our human creativity, we have become aware that we are part of a global ecosystem, in which the impact of the species *homo sapiens* has led us from one point of no return to another, to where we are now. Although nostalgia for the return to a Golden Age is as old as the human race, we have lost our innocence and our garden of Eden. Whatever we say and do, whatever we do not say and do, it has a desired outcome and an undesired one. It starts to belong to the non-teleological development of the human race, which belongs to the physical, biological and cultural domains. Dumas[13] wrote that the basic attitude of system thinkers and practitioners is humility before the autonomy of the living systems under scrutiny.

This last controversy reduces to an operational value statement. It helps me to understand and to act relevantly on 'global' issues. I see it as an antidote against the preponderant political and media message, which finally leads only to a sense of powerlessness, of dependency and counterdependency, of a tendency to point to culprits and scapegoats.

Perhaps it is worth illustrating consequences of this last controversy in the three domains.

In the added-value domain I help my clients to discover the reason for the existence of the work systems in which they participate. I mentioned earlier that one of the most powerful tools to achieve this is to discover who their clients are and which qualities they appreciate. But most work systems are only a link in a chain which starts from the initial processing of a raw material to the final consumption of products or services. Big business has tried to encompass the whole chain by what is called 'vertical integration'. This has led to unmanageable systems. I say to my clients that it is always worth understanding the requirements of the clients of their clients but that it becomes a futile exercise to try to go beyond that. The only hope I can give them is that if everyone in the chain is concerned to fulfil the expectations of their clients in relation to their clients' clients, the chain as a whole works and the added value from their activities is guaranteed.

Although I have stressed the quality of systemicity of innovations, there is always a risk involved in changing the rules of the game. For any innovation, desired or undesired, outcomes are bound to occur, new beneficiaries and new victims are unavoidable. When innovating groups become aware of the uncertainties related to this risk I help them to keep track of the relations they have with their major stakeholders. The hope I can give them is that as long as the new rules of the game encourage the mutually satisfactory relations with these stakeholders to be continued, the risk is worth taking. But hope is never a guarantee.

When I am working with people involved in activities in the value-systems domain my major preoccupation is with the congruency of the people with whom I am working. The major risk in the value systems domain is that people become depersonalized, they start to be 'speakers' for others, they become ideological propagandists. The quality of the personal relations between the various representatives is the best check on the quality of the work done in the referent group.

The universal value of persons operating in the spiritual domain resides in the humble expressions of their internal riches.

In fact, these four examples illustrate a basic tenet of systemic thinking and systemic practice.

One can start from any well-defined system, intervene and contribute to its development, as long as one takes into account its major interfaces with its direct environment. In human activity systems or work systems, this reduces to permanent attention and care for the major stakeholders of the system. One cannot change a system without changing its relation with its environment. This is the humble base of global action through local focus and attention.

I have developed this last controversy because it provides me with an alternative understanding of what happens in the political and the value-systems domain following current discourse, which is based on the definition of social systems as aggregates. The only way to look through the discourse which uses classifications for balancing power is to point to the systemic nature of power relations.

When someone raised the issue that, in 20 years, 35% of the inhabitants of Amsterdam will be allochtones (a friendly word for 'strangers') I asked him what allochtones could mean when they formed the majority of the inhabitants. Either Amsterdam will be a different city, where the distinction between auto- and allochtones will have lost its impact, or it will be a city at war, when the ideological distinction between allochtones and autochtones is maintained.

It came rather as a shock to an Irish friend who took part in a referent search conference in the United States on the issue of Northern Ireland when I asked him why the British Army had not been invited as a major stakeholder. After so many years, they must have a stake in the issue and will have something to lose when the issue is settled. The Army is a system in its own right and not just an executive arm of the body politic. No peace treaty has ever been signed without dealing with its consequence for the armies involved.

Even so, a lawyer friend was also rather shocked when I referred to the idealistic background of the separation of powers in our democracies. Legislative, juridical and executive power have to be intertwined if one of them wants to be able to perform. In fact, they are intertwined, through long-standing personal relations. Russian citizens look rather sceptically at the 'as if' problem between their president and the parliament, who are trying to apply the separation of powers in practice.

I leave it to the reader to look further at the political realm in terms of local systems of interpersonal relations instead of abstract power relations between social aggregates that are more or less arbitrarily defined by someone.

Controversy 9: On governance

I repeat my definition of activities in the value-systems domain: those activities which create the necessary infrastructure for bringing representatives of different value systems together and for maintaining fertile debates between them, which in their turn can lead to innovations. In fact, these are essentially political activities. They can be found in any area of human activity and are not limited to what is formally defined as the realm of politics.

On the other hand, many activities which formally belong to the realm of politics can be analysed in terms of innovations or added-value activities. The public–private dichotomy in relation to the activities done by work systems is irrelevant. There is no direct relation between formal ownership, which belongs to the domain of power relations, and the performance of work systems.

I showed in Controversy 3 how in the framework which I developed ownership is a relation, not a position. The nature of the work and the network of interpersonal relations in which the work system is embedded defines ownership relations. Hence in private and public enterprises, as in the body politic, there are two perspectives from which governance can be viewed:

- 'Governors' or 'managers' or 'leaders' act as if they have to keep together the people whom they want to govern. I call this the family perspective.
- 'Governors' or 'managers' or 'leaders' are contributing to a shared desired outcome of the work systems which they 'govern', 'manage' or 'lead'. This contribution is related to the domain to which the work system belongs. I call this the work perspective.

Again, these two statements are value statements. It is clear from the focus of this book which one I prefer. Nevertheless, in all human history, in all kinds of institutions which were and are still viable, there has been a dialectical relation between both perspectives. Governance in the value-systems domain implies the continuing debate between the two legitimate perspectives. They are directly related to a tension which is fully human between

- The desire to belong to a group, to maintain the group and to take care of it. This is a centripetal perspective; and
- The desire to do something together, to express the reason for the existence of the group in products, services, innovations, languages, works of art, institutions, behaviour—in short, to do work. This is a centrifugal perspective.

Many of the actual social pathologies with which we are now confronted result from either the denial of one of the perspectives or the confusing of both perspectives in ideological discourses.

Nationalism and, in general, every fundamentalism as an ideology is a perversion of the first desire. This perversion lies in the substitution of a system of real interpersonal relations by an abstraction, 'Collective Man' as Toynbee[14] rightly pointed out, is 'Not what I do or what the other does is important, only who I am and who the other is'. As a consequence, the pathological work governed by this ideology is war, the destruction of the other.

For this reason, I have become very critical of all kinds of discourse in organizations or the political field which take aggregated classifications of people as realities: the unemployed, the rich, the politicians, the Third World, the nation, etc. They have the seeds of war in them. For the same reason, the economic discourse in politics which speaks of the Wealth of Nations ultimately expresses itself in destruction: waste of people, natural resources, values and work. Only when the reason for the existence for someone else, the customer, the quality of life of the others, the quality of the environment, in short, the survival of the ecosystem, counterbalances this discourse are valuable dialectics restored.

Performance and economic efficiency as an ideology is a perversion of the second desire. This perversion lies in the substitution of a system of activities embedded in a system of relations by an abstraction, an External Goal. It is not important who I am or who the other is, only my output or the output of the other. As a consequence, the pathological work governed by this ideology becomes infighting, ostracism, the breaking of interpersonal relations and, ultimately, self-destruction.

Therefore I have become very critical of all kinds of discourse in organizations or in the political field which refer to absolute goals: 'scientific truth', progress, duty, necessary change, efficiency, survival, etc. They have the seeds of self-destruction in them: waste of people, natural resources, values and a sense of community. Only when the care for my colleagues, the care and the maintenance of the tools I use, the care for the material I use, in short, the survival of the ecosystem, counterbalances this discourse, will valuable dialectics be restored.

The advantage of looking at ethics and value systems from these two perspectives lies in the fact that the ultimate reference to the outcome belongs not to the world of ideas but to our relationship with our social, biological and physical environment. If we see around us physical, biological and social destruction (and, as human beings, we will always be confronted with them) we can start to restore the lost balance in our models, theories and value systems.

This balance is the core of all debates which take place between 'governors' in the value-systems domain and in the political, economic, social and cultural realms. In any case, it helps me to sort out the ideological mess or the bogus debates, which are no more than mere propaganda. Propaganda—political, economical, social and cultural—is the method used to close for each of us the feedback loop between what we see with our eyes, what we hear with our ears, what we smell with our nose, what we taste with our tongue, what we feel with our skin and what we sense as human beings, related to our own physical, biological and social environment. Ideology is a surrogate for simple human empiricism.

If 'governors' are out of touch with themselves, they are out of touch with everything and no longer deserve the name 'governor' in any domain.

This last controversy is virtually a poem: it summarizes where I stand. In a certain sense, this last controversy with which I am struggling and will probably do so for the rest of my life, is the path which leads me into the spiritual domain. It is the path I am looking forward to, through my encounters with the works of art of contemporary spiritual artists or with this part of the mystery of the spiritual traditions, which I dare to understand.

REFERENCES

1. Mintzberg, H. (1979). *The Structuring of Organizations*, Prentice Hall
2. Smith, A. (1776). *The Wealth of Nations*, Penguin Classics (1986)
3. Samuelson, P. (1964). *Economics*, McGraw-Hill
4. Porter, M. (1990). *The Competitive Advantage of Nations*, Free Press
5. Maturana, U. and Varela, F. (1987). *The Tree of Knowledge*, Shambhala Publications
6. Piore, J.M. and Sabel, Ch. F. (1984). *The Second Industrial Divide*, Basic Books
7. Handy, C. (1984). *The Future of Work*, Dutch translation (1986), Bruna & Zoon
8. Mintzberg, H. (1983). *Power in and around Organizations*, Prentice Hall
9. Lenat, D. (1982). The nature of heuristics, *Artificial Intelligence*, **19**, North-Holland
10. Touraine, A. (1969). *La Société Post-industrielle*, Editions Denoël
11. Galbraith, J.K. (1992). *The Culture of Contentment*, Houghton Mifflin
12. Beer, S. (1975). *Platform for Change*, Wiley
13. Dumas, Ph. (1976). *General System Theory, A Behavioural Approach*, Institut d'Administration des Entreprises, Aix-en-Provence
14. Toynbee, A. (1963). *A Study of History*, Oxford University Press

Chapter 9

——— Annotated Bibliography and Conclusions

The two books by Stafford Beer which have helped me most to start thinking in terms of the Viable Systems Model are *The Brain of the Firm*, Wiley, 1981, and *The Heart of Enterprise*, Wiley, 1979. Later he published *Diagnosing the System for Organizations*, Wiley, 1985.

Although the last is apparently more didactic, it requires much more self-discipline from the reader. For those who are interested in having an overview of several applications of the VSM, I recommend *The Viable System Model*, edited by Raul Espejo and Roger Harnden, Wiley, 1990.

Apart from the *Journal of Applied Systems Analysis*, published by the University of Lancaster, where one can find how Soft Systems Methodology is developing, and the journal *Systems Practice*, published by Plenum Press, New York and London, which positions Beer and Checkland in the stream of Systems Thinking, the following works develop SSM:

Peter Checkland, *Systems Thinking, Systems Practice*, Wiley, 1981
Peter Checkland and Jim Scholes, *Soft Systems Methodology in Action*, Wiley, 1990
Brian Wilson, *Systems: Concepts, Methodologies and Applications*, Wiley, 1984.

The works of Elliott Jaques which have influenced me most are
A General Theory of Bureaucracy, Heineman, 1983, and *The Form of Time*, Heineman, 1982. You may like his latest work, *Requisite Organization*, Cason Hall, 1989. I was disappointed with this because Jaques apparently could not use his findings on time span coherently. He is still obsessed by the monolithic organizational paradigm.

I am pleased that even economists begin to understand the networklike behaviour of markets and firms, instead of seeing them as aggregates of autonomous actors working with their individual preferences. They seem also to be able to make the distinction between added-value domain economies and innovation economies. I recommend two works which were useful for me to make my case with economists: Michael Piore and Charles

Sabel, *The Second Industrial Divide*, Basic Books, 1983, and Michael Best, *The New Competition*, Polity Press, 1990.

Geoffrey Vickers has inspired me most to understand activities in the value-systems domain. His *The Art of Judgment*, Harper and Row, 1983 is invaluable. As an introduction to his thinking I must mention the article by P. Checkland and A. Casar, Vickers' concept of an appreciative system: a systemic account, *Journal of Applied Systems Analysis*, **13**, 1986.

The development of the concept of the Referent Organization can be found in Eric Trist, Referent organizations and the development of inter-organizational domains, lecture to the Academy of Management, 39th Annual Convention, Atlanta, 1979. Until Beer's *Team Tensegrity* (Wiley) appears, an experience of a referent search conference can be found in David Schecter, Beer's 'Organizational Tensegrity' and the challenge of democratic management, *Systems Practice*, **4**, No. 4, 1991.

Two authors who have influenced me greatly are Maturana and Varela. They have, in my opinion, created openings in the futile debate between structuralists, who claim that there are invariant structures, separated from an observer, and the social constructionists, who state that everything is in the language. This debate remains futile as long as ideas are reified. The epistemological statements of Maturana and Varela that knowing is doing and doing is knowing, and that everything said is said by someone, transcend this dichotomy and, even more, give an epistemological basis for what 'science' may start to mean in the twenty-first century. Empiricism can then be redefined as the restored relation of actors between what they do and what they experience as participant observers. Thinking and practice are inseparable.

In *Autopoiesis and Cognition, the Realization of the Living*, D. Reidel, 1980, Maturana and Varela develop in a very rigorous way their epistemology. In *The Tree of Knowledge*, Shambhala Press, 1987, they word their findings in an apparently easier way. But because their theory has immediate behavioural implications, it is clearly a value-laden theory, and reading it in whatever form will remain difficult.

One of the discoveries I made while writing this book is that the process never ends. In 'scientific' papers it is the custom to express this by referring to directions for further research. As this book reflects a practitioner's practice, finally I would like to point out the directions for future actions which have emerged during my writing:

- It has become clear to me that there is an urgent demand for rethinking the whole domain of economic theory. To escape from the ideological straightjacket in which this thinking is bound I wish to relate again to 'real' economic transactions between 'real' partners. The way the barter and the black economy are working, the way economic activities still take place in hyperinflationary circumstances is the ground for empirical action. But also under normal economic circumstances, inside large organizations the framework I have developed can help to define the added value of the various work systems, which provide products and services to internal customers. These are also economic transactions. The concepts of transfer prices, of profit and loss centres are becoming increasingly less relevant when intra- and inter-organizational interdependencies become more important. In practice, the definition of the added value of a work system by its customers in terms of throughput time, intrinsic quality, volume, and the effort the customer is prepared to spend to benefit from the products and services of the supplier work system leads to a more manageable economic domain. Fewer figures, more facts lead to fewer accountants and more managers. This will become the focus of my practice in the added-value domain.

- In the innovation domain I spend much energy as a practitioner enhancing the attributes of the transferability and systemicity of the results of innovative effort. Hence, innovation means considerably more than technological innovation. Social and institutional innovations are much more relevant in tackling the issues with which we are confronted at the end of this century: underdevelopment, the environment, international legal incompetence, war and crime. These innovations are often helped by returning to the original rationale and purpose of the institutions and organizations, which now seem to be dysfunctioning. After having spoken with colleagues about my perspective of the innovation domain and its emergent characteristics, I received the feedback that their clients (technological research or health care research institutes) were able to use the model for debating previously irreconcilable issues. I am myself involved in the review of the financing mechanisms of a large research institute and I am agreeably surprised how the model creates a positive dynamic in the institute and in the business units, which are its potential clients and its actual stakeholders, even on the delicate issue of who will have to pay for the research.

- From the experiences which I mentioned when I developed the concepts of the value-systems domain, my major work concerns local authorities and regional development. All large institutions are now under pressure. Ideological discourses on the corruptive nature of power are not very helpful for people who have their democratic heart in the right place. Working from the grass roots upwards seems to me the most adequate path for reform. I was surprised to find when I started to focus upon regional development how many successful experiments there are. From Togo and Bilbao to Poland and Slovenia, a new kind of political action is taking place, which is the harbinger of the democracies of tomorrow. They make their errors but do not claim to be perfect, which is perhaps the best position they can take. I have lost all hope for the big 'machines': big government, big business and big crime are self-defeating. My optimism resides in the fact that viable systems are extremely resilient and are able to cope with pathologies.

- Finally, concerning the spiritual domain, I will increasingly actively search for artists or other people who will confront me with the basic dilemmas of all human beings. As Maturana wrote:

porqué la muerte es la muerte
y tras la muerte està la vida
que sin la muerte solo es muerte.

Because death is death
and beyond death there is life
which without death is only death.

Here we are at the end of our journey. I hope that by now you have the flavour of what can be described and prescribed by the framework developed in previous chapters. In any case, this language helps me in making human activities more transparent to myself and to the people with whom I am working. The framework helps me to put in practice a motto I read in one of Stafford Beer's books:

Look at what the system does, don't listen to what it says it does.

Although I am convinced that playing games is an essential human activity and is one of the foundations for building workable relations between people, my engineering prejudice tells me that in terms of the real needs with which our world and its 5 billion people are confronted, the relationship between the efforts invested in play and in work is out of balance. Perhaps starting to play with the conceptual framework I have developed may, paradoxically, help you to restore this balance. Good luck!

Chapter 10
Synopsis and Glossary

Figure 10.1 gives an overview of the structure of this book. It will help you to position a specific definition, which is written in italics within the summary of the corresponding chapter.

CHAPTER 1 BACKGROUND AND PURPOSE

This book aims to describe a conceptual framework that is relevant for understanding and intervening in the task-related issues of work systems. The value behind the framework and part of its aims is to relate human activities again with identifiable human beings.

CHAPTER 2 BASIC CONCEPTS OF THE FRAMEWORK

2.1 Concepts Referring to the Work System Itself

2.1.1 The Work System

A work system is a purposeful definition of the real world in which people spend effort in more or less coherent activities for mutually influencing each other and their environment.

2.1.2 Transformation Process

A transformation process expresses a basic purpose behind the work system and transforms a specified input into a specified output. The output must contain the input which has been transformed during the process.

2.1.3 Process Level

A process of a higher order is one whose output creates conditions for one of a lower order. Processes can be differentiated in a hierarchy. To avoid confusion with what is seen in organizational terms as hierarchical levels we call this the process level (Figure 2.1).

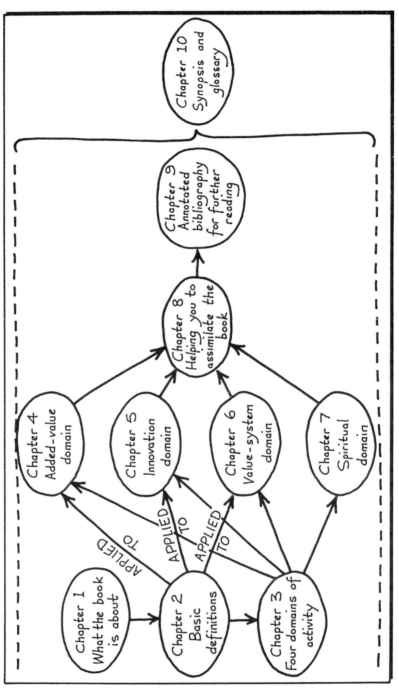

Figure 10.1   The structure of this book

2.1.4 Contributions of People

We call contributions those activities of people belonging to a work system which can be seen as helping to realize the defined output of a process. The process level defines the level of the contribution at the same time.

2.1.5 Responsibility and Accountability

One can be held responsible only for one's own contributions to a process. As a formal simplifying mechanism it may be useful to have someone accountable for the process and its output. In this way responsibilities and accountabilities become nominally known. Anonymous entities such as organizations, departments, institutions, groups, governments, etc. can be held neither responsible nor accountable.

2.1.7 Clients, Actors, Owners: the Major Stakeholders of the Process

Those who contribute to the realization of the output of the process are assuming the actor's role. Those who are the beneficiaries or the victims of the output of the process are adopting the client's role. Those who can effectively decide to stop the process are assuming the owner's role.

2.1.8 Environmental Constraints and Weltanschauung

Environmental constraints are boundaries which are taken as immutable. They cannot be influenced but nevertheless are worth mentioning. Weltanschauung is the implicit perspective which makes the definition of a process meaningful for the various parties involved.

2.1.9 The Management Process

Management consists of those contributions which transform the transactions of a process with its environment into a coherent pattern so that all the parties involved in the process—actors, clients and owners—are enabled to identify that process, its purpose and the development of its purpose. Management essentially is about meaning.

2.2 Relations between Work Systems and Processes: Information Processes

Information is the raw material for creating and conveying meaning, thus for management.

2.2.1 Strategic Information Processes

All information processes which contribute to management, we call strategic information processes. These create, convey and develop meaning to all people involved in a work system.

Ideally, strategic information processes lead to a shared meaning about the processes to be managed among the people managing them. Debate between people and the dialectics between their perspectives is the only form of strategic information process. If contradiction and dissension cease between the people in a work system, it is then doomed to failure and usually creates victims when it fails.

2.2.2 Control Information Processes

Control information processes are those which lead to a corrective, regulative action by the people contributing to transformation processes. Control information flows through a corrective feedback loop (Figure 2.3).

2.2.3 Information Processes for Understanding the Work System or Audit Information Processes

Audit information processes are those which lead the actors to a more profound understanding of why the process is carried out, what it does, with what means it is performed and how these means are used.

2.3 Process Levels and Time Span

time span, i.e. the time needed to materialize the results of activities deployed.

2.4 Span of Relations as a Constraint on the Size of Work Systems

The span of relations is the maximum number of people able to attribute a shared meaning to the system of relations they develop through the system of activities in which they are involved:

(1) The small group, with a maximum of nine people: the creative group.
(2) The large group with a maximum of about 80 people: the reflective group.
(3) The adaptive group with a maximum of about 700 people.

CHAPTER 3 THE FOUR DOMAINS: DEFINITION AND GENERAL CHARACTERISTICS

3.1 First Approach

3.2 The Story of the Four Stonemasons

3.3 Relating Recursion Levels with the Domains

In a recursive organizational structure any viable system contains and is contained in a viable system.

3.4 Structure of the Chapters on Each Domain

CHAPTER 4 THE ADDED-VALUE DOMAIN: FROM A TIME SPAN OF ONE DAY TO ONE OF 2 YEARS

4.1 Basic Description of the Domain

A set of relatively homogeneous requirements of a group of clients are transformed into those requirements being met so that clients, owners and actors can appreciate the relevance of the work system. In the added-value domain added and subtracted value is created for its clients, actors and owners alike.

4.1.1 Throughput Time

This is the time between the formulation of the requirement of the client until it is met to his or her satisfaction.

4.1.2 Volume Requirements

The volume is the number of items of a product or a service that are seen as a relevant unit for the customer.

4.1.3 Quality Requirements

The intrinsic quality of a product or service is the emergent systemic quality in which the customer places his or her appreciation of the product or service.

4.1.4 Price Requirements

The appreciation that the client has for a certain product or service is directly related to the price he or she is prepared to pay for it. This price can be expressed by money, goods or services, which require effort.

4.2 Process Level or Stratum 1: from 1 Day to 3 Months

4.2.1. Generic Transformation Process

To materialize a specified output (product, service or a combination of both) with a prescribed means, technology and method, in the most efficient way, i.e. with a minimum of waste. Efficiency is defined here (cf. Checkland[3]) as the realization of the process with a minimum of wasted means.

4.2.2 Basic Strategic Dilemma

Can the required output be realized with a minimum of waste? The demand for efficiency for meeting a defined client requirement with the tools and methods at hand is satisfied in the processes taking place at this process level. Nowhere else can efficiency be achieved.

4.2.3 Control Information

There is a need to have a direct feedback about the present state of the required output and the waste produced in the process.

4.2.4 Audit Information

Reviewing the understanding of the output specifications and the standard procedures to achieve them and the analysis of waste patterns generated in the process.

4.2.5 Development Activities

Debating the relevance of the several specifications to learn what are minimal critical specifications of the output, the input and the process itself, leading to more efficient work.

4.3 Process Level 2: from 3 Months to 1 Year

4.3.1 Generic Transformation Process

To mould the specific requirements of the clients of the processes on process level 1 into minimal critical specifications regarding the output, the procedures, the tools and the input for those who perform the activities on level 1.

Parenthesis 1: Short- and long-term allocation of capital.
Parenthesis 2: Employment and other macro-economic schemes.

4.3.2 Basic Strategic Dilemma

Are the inputs to the process, the procedures and the tools still the best for meeting the client's specific requirements? The basic questions of efficacy (Checkland [3]) have to be asked here. Are we using the right means to achieve the result aimed at, the fulfilment of the client's requirements?

4.3.3 Control Information

Two feedback loops must be monitored permanently. One relates to the transformation of the client's requirement in workable specifications. The other refers to the efficacy of the work system, the adequacy of the means used to achieve the output specifications.

4.3.4 Audit Information

Here we can introduce the regular diagnostic procedures described in Section 2.2.3. The focus of the understanding of these processes must be on the fit between the resources made available to process level 1 and an understanding of the client's requirements.

4.3.5 Development Activities

All projects which lead to an improvement of specifications and the resources available on process level 1 belong here.

4.4 Process level 3: from 1 to 2 years

The added-value domain encompasses the realm of economic activities. When one looks from the perspective of work systems, one only sees small and medium-sized businesses in the profit and non-profit sectors, which have as basic aims to maintain mutually satisfactory relations with major stakeholders, customers, suppliers and employees. These relations express themselves in products, services and money. These are the byproducts of the activities, which conserve and adapt the relational structure between the stakeholders.

4.4.1 Generic Transformation Process

Developing alternative products and services and alternative ways of meeting the requirements and needs of known clients. Taking care of the right balance between ends and means.

4.4.2 Basic Strategic Dilemma

Choices have to be made to allocate means for alternative products and services for known clients and ways of meeting the needs of those chosen clients. How far and how late do we react to developments in our environment?

4.4.3 Control Information

A systematic follow-up to see if our procedures, tools, machines, processes, inputs and outputs are starting to show 'strange behaviour'.

4.4.4 Audit Information

For the first time, purely internal audits are no longer sufficient. There is a need for regular (once a year or every two years) attendance at trade fairs, conferences, etc. to understand whether the activities deployed within the operational domain still match what is happening outside it.

4.4.5 Development Activities

On this level we improve and adapt our products and services systematically and, if relevant, change our ways of providing them in terms of well-tested technologies and methods.

4.5 Applications and Interventions in the Added-value Domain

4.5.1 Defining Product Lines from the Viewpoint of Customers

4.5.2 Process Analysis for Improving the Efficiency of Operations

CHAPTER 5 THE SECOND RECURSION LEVEL: THE INNOVATION DOMAIN

5.1 Basic Description of the Innovation Domain

Changes in values in the environment in which the work system in the innovation domain is embedded are sensed and transformed into new products, services and processes. The work system is involved in the discovery and the creation of the added value of the future.

5.1.1 Desirability

Desirability then becomes an attribute of a relation between innovators and stakeholders. It can be measured by the degree of positive effort that both make in that relation.

5.1.2 Feasibility

Here again, feasibility is an attribute of the relation between innovators and *stakeholders. It can be measured by the degree of defensive effort that both invest in the relation.*

5.1.3 Transferability

The degree to which an innovation can easily be spread in the added-value domain gives an indication of its transferability.

5.1.4 Systemicity

The degree in which an innovation has been conceived, taking into account the interfaces with other areas, is an indicator of its systemicity.

5.2 Process Level 3: from 1 to 2 Years

Basic strategic dilemma: choices have to be made to allocate resources for alternative products and services for known clients and alternative ways of meeting the needs of those chosen clients. How far and how late do we react to developments in the environment?

Choices have to be made for alternative products and services in which known clients could be interested. Do we take the risk of reformulating the needs of those clients through these novel products or services?

5.3 Process Level 4: from 2 to 5 Years

5.3.1 Generic Transformation Process

Transforming the signals of change in the value systems of the major stakeholders into new generic products and services which at the same time make this change perceptible to them. They reveal concretely the future which is already present and shape it in that way.

5.3.2 Basic Strategic Dilemma

Attachment to or detachment from what already exists is the dilemma confronted by innovators active on recursion level 4.

5.3.3 Control Information

The reaction of the stakeholders and the timely detection of new stakeholders have to be monitored.

5.3.4 Audit Information

This is the first audit which has to ask whether the systems in the operational domain are really doing what they say, and whether we understand the meaning behind any discrepancy, based upon our knowledge of changing value systems.

5.3.5 Development Activities

Activities whose objective is to introduce and disseminate innovative products and services belong to this level.

Parenthesis: Research.

5.4 Process Level 5: from 5 to 10 Years

5.4.1 Generic Transformation Process

Sensing the changes in value systems, to recreate conceptually whole systems which reflect these changes and thus to create conditions for the introduction of innovative products and services relevant to these changes. On this level the rules of the game for the next decade are consciously made.

5.4.2 Basic Strategic Dilemma

Although immediate results are not available to verify choices, the efforts deployed on this level create a point of no return—in technical terms, a bifurcation point.

5.4.3 Control Information

Do we follow up the development of the meaning that the various stakeholders involved in the transformation process attribute to this process?

5.4.4 Audit Information

How far do the stakeholders of an innovation still adhere to the values which were the basis of their decision to transform a whole system?

5.4.5. Development Activities

These activities aim at whole-system transformations. In business terms this results in the creation of whole new product/service/market/technology combinations. In more general terms this signifies the creation of a new network of relations between stakeholders who were previously unknown to each other or whose relations were completely different.

5.5 Applications and Interventions in the Innovation Domain

CHAPTER 6 THE THIRD RECURSION LEVEL: THE VALUE-SYSTEMS DOMAIN

6.1 Basic Description of the Domain

The value-systems domain is involved in the permanent creation of the elements of a new culture by creating new languages and new descriptions and prescriptions about the world through a permanent debate between the carriers of different world views, traditions and cultures.

   Political activities refer to interactions between proponents of different value systems, not to achieve a certain form of consensus or compromise, but to agree that it is worth continuing the debate and its underlying relations.

6.1.1 Generative

Generative theories empower their users to develop a new repertoire of behaviour, of ways to deal with their natural and cultural environment.

6.1.2 Tolerant

Tolerance means that although I cannot agree with certain world views or values, I do not judge their proponents or try to eliminate them. Acceptance means that I no longer make an effort to change a state of affairs which goes directly against my world view and values.

6.1.3 Dialectical

Adversaries have a trusting relation. Although their values and world views may be completely contradictory, nevertheless they appreciate and trust each other as human beings.

6.1.4 Congruent

Persons taking part in debates which create new value systems are personally involved and have the difficult task of recreating their own world views. If they are not thoroughly grounded in their own humanity and its traditions, if they have not creatively integrated these traditions in their own lives, they risk their own personality in the debate. The debate requires and strengthens the congruency between the inner and outer worlds of the participants.

6.2 Process Level 5: from 5 to 10 Years

Basic strategic dilemma: A whole-system innovation creates a bifurcation point, a point of no return. Through the assessment of the consequences of the innovation, the value-system behind it is challenged. The innovation implies the change of the innovator. He or she can accept or reject the 'parenthood' of the innovation.

6.3 Process Level 6: from 10 to 20 Years

6.3.1 Generic Transformation Process

In a given area of human activities, members of referent groups debate their 'appreciative systems' and thus create a coherent language about their area for stimulating activities in the innovation domain.

6.3.2 Basic Strategic Dilemma

The creation of new value systems and languages is 'abstract' and has an 'idealistic' flavour. The tension between ideology and value systems is continuously present.

6.3.3 Control Information

When referent groups are able to manage their membership in terms of the relevance of the debate, they are self-regulated. Membership assessment should be undertaken at least every two years or, more frequently, annually to provide steering information.

6.3.4 Audit Information

The way the referent groups are spoken of in the innovation and added-value domains, the respect they deserve is the major warning to avoid the fate of many of them to become an 'old boy's network', whose members seem to have lost touch with their own environment.

6.3.5 Development Activities

On this process level development becomes non-teleological.

6.4 Process Level 7: from 20 to 50 Years

6.4.1 Generic Transformation Process

On this process level a language and values are developed which encompass many areas of human activity. Cultures are also developed. A culture can be defined as a broad aggregation of people who share the same 'appreciative system', the same value language.

6.4.2 Basic Strategic Dilemma

The development of a new culture is bound to use the existing language of the 'Establishment'. Nevertheless, it changes the context of its usage. The tension between rupture and displacement has to be managed.

6.5 Applications and Interventions in the Value-systems Domain

6.5.1 Basic Principles of the Mondragon Co-operative Experience

6.5.2 Proposal for a Search Conference for Defining Projects for Regional Development

6.6 Appreciation, Appreciative Systems and Appreciative Enquiry

CHAPTER 7 BEYOND THE 20-YEAR TIME SPAN: THE SPIRITUAL DOMAIN

7.1 Generic Transformation Process

To materialize through works of art or mere behaviour the universal understanding of one's own mortality.

7.2 Basic Strategic Dilemma

To struggle with one's own consciousness of death in a creative way. To live with and live beyond the depression of the loneliness associated with working through one's own death by creating universally recognizable expressions of human life and death.

CHAPTER 8 STARTING TO PLAY WITH THE FRAMEWORK

8.1 Personal Reflection Upon Your Own Work and Contributions

8.2 A Controversial Blueprint of the World of Work

Controversy 1: Economics

8.2.1 Relations between Work Systems in the Added-value Domain

Controversy 2: Competition

Free markets are much more collaborative than competitive ones and, exactly for that reason, more economic. Competition is the game played within the constraints of collaborative relationships.

Controversy 3: Ownership

The most important owners of work systems in the added-value domain are their clients. Then follow the actors. When the formal owners, the shareholders, are not actors in the work system, they are the least important stakeholders and do not deserve the name of 'owner'.

8.2.2 Relations between Work Systems in the Added-value and Innovation Domains

Controversy 4: There is never a need for innovations

8.2.3 Relations between the Work Systems in the Innovation Domain

Controversy 5: Planning versus innovation

What is normally understood as planning is incompatible with the concept of innovation. Hence, planning in innovative projects now means for me the joint elaboration by the actors in a project of the logic of the activities which can be used to debate the status of complex systems of interrelated activities with an uncertain outcome and with unpredictable mutual feedback loops and non-linear mutual causalities.

8.2.4 Relations between Work Systems in the Innovation and Value-systems Domains and those in the Value-systems Domain

Controversy 6: Making the news.
Controversy 7: The scale of representative democracies.
Controversy 8: Global through local.
Controversy 9: On governance.

Index

Note: Page references in *italics* refer to figures

Index compiled by Annette Musker